GIANTS

July 2013

Welcome to the Northwest!

Cathy & Jerry

GIANTS

THE COLOSSAL TREES OF PACIFIC NORTH AMERICA

Audrey Grescoe

Photography by Bob Herger

ROBERTS RINEHART PUBLISHERS

International Standard Book Number 1-57098-169-8

Library of Congress Number 97-68071

Published by Roberts Rinehart Publishers
5455 Spine Road
Boulder, Colorado 80301

First published in 1997 by Raincoast Books

Distributed to the trade by Publishers Group West

1 2 3 4 5 6 7 8 9 10

Designed by Dean Allen
Project Editor: Michael Carroll
Copy Editor: Rachelle Kanefsky
Map by Eric Leinberger

Printed and bound in Hong Kong through Palace Press International

For Paul, who envisioned and believed

Contents

Fog creeps into a Sitka spruce forest bringing life-sustaining nutrients and moisture.

Acknowledgments

FOR TAKING THE TIME to explain their work and for vetting drafts, I am particularly grateful to Robert Duncan and Alan K. Mitchell of the Canadian Forest Service; Michael Carlson, John Russell, and Jack Woods at the Research Branch of the B.C. Ministry of Forests; Thomas Hinkley and Robert Van Pelt at the University of Washington; Nalini Nadkarni at Evergreen State College; Peter McAuliffe at Scott Paper; Cees van Oosten at MacMillan Bloedel; and Chuck Lockhart at K Ply. W. H. Moir, research ecologist, USDA Forest Service, in Flagstaff, Arizona, read the entire manuscript and made many suggestions that helped to clarify the text.

For responding warmly and generously to requests for information, I am indebted to Bill Beese at MacMillan Bloedel; Al and Mary Carder; Robert Hagel and Tara Sahota of the Canadian Forest Service; Pam Kranitz of the Canadian Wildlife Service; Lara Lamport of the Ecoforestry Institute in Victoria; Andy MacKinnon, Jim Pojar, and Cheng C. Ying at the B.C. Ministry of Forests; Richard Ring and Neville Winchester at the University of Victoria; and Hans Roemer of the B.C. Ministry of Environment, Lands, and Parks.

Americans who came to my aid included John Alden at the Institute of Northern Forestry; Martha Benioff of the Save-the-Redwoods League; Collen Dement of the Public Forestry Foundation; Gary McCausland at Fort Lewis, Washington; Stephen Underwood at Redwood National Park; Olympic National Park ranger Mary Dessel and information officer Barb Maynes; and, in the USDA Forest Service, Tom Conkle in California, Debra Warren and Neil McKay in Oregon, Larry Frank in Washington, and Ken Wright in Alaska.

Thanks also to John Bese, Larry Courchaine, Curtis Erpelding, Brian Hoover, Reid Hudson, Will Koop, Kevin Maher, Cornelia Oberlander, Eric Redekop, and Isaac Tait whose concern for trees is heartening; to Mark Budgen, who allowed me extended loans from his comprehensive personal library; to numerous patient librarians at the B.C. Ministry of Forests, the Vancouver Public Library, the University of British Columbia Faculty of Forestry, and the Fort Vancouver Regional Library in Washington State; and to George Brandak, the manuscripts curator in Special Collections at the University of British Columbia.

The seed cone of the Douglas fir, distinguished by a three-pronged bract protruding from its scales, grows upward during pollination but bends downward while its seeds are being dispersed.

And to Bob Herger, who cared more about this project than an author might have reasonably expected, I owe a great deal of gratitude.

A special word of appreciation must also go to Rachelle Kanefsky for her copyediting, and to Michael Carroll for his attentive structural editing and his professional diplomacy in helping control my pedantic tendencies. On his advice I have acceded to an editorial decision to use the familiar spellings of the common names of certain trees, even though current forestry texts use hyphenated or one-word variations to indicate, for example, that a Douglas-fir is not a fir or that a western redcedar is not a cedar.

x

—

GIANTS

Found within 180 miles of the Pacific coast, bigleaf maples are islands of open, dappled light in predominantly coniferous forests.

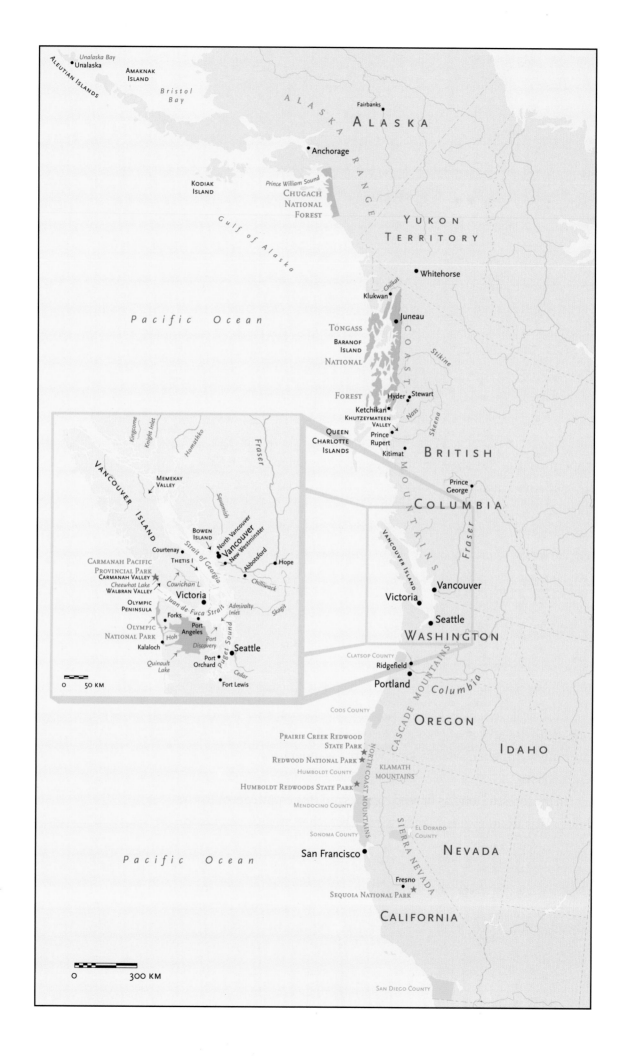

Unalaska Bay
• Unalaska
ALEUTIAN ISLANDS
AMAKNAK ISLAND
Bristol Bay

ALASKA RANGE
ALASKA
Fairbanks •

• Anchorage

KODIAK ISLAND
Prince William Sound
CHUGACH NATIONAL FOREST

YUKON TERRITORY

Gulf of Alaska

Pacific Ocean

• Whitehorse
Chilkat
Klukwan •
TONGASS
• Juneau
BARANOF ISLAND
Stikine
NATIONAL
COAST
FOREST
Hyder • Stewart
Ketchikan •
KHUTZEYMATEEN VALLEY
Nass
QUEEN CHARLOTTE ISLANDS
Prince Rupert •
Skeena
• Kitimat
BRITISH

Prince George •
MOUNTAINS
COLUMBIA

Fraser
VANCOUVER ISLAND

Vancouver •
Victoria •
Seattle •
WASHINGTON

CLATSOP COUNTY
Ridgefield •
Portland •
Columbia
CASCADE MOUNTAINS
OREGON

COOS COUNTY
IDAHO

PRAIRIE CREEK REDWOOD STATE PARK ★
REDWOOD NATIONAL PARK ★
NORTH COAST MOUNTAINS
HUMBOLDT COUNTY
KLAMATH MOUNTAINS
HUMBOLDT REDWOODS STATE PARK ★
MENDOCINO COUNTY

EL DORADO COUNTY
SONOMA COUNTY
SIERRA NEVADA
NEVADA

Pacific Ocean
San Francisco •

Fresno •
SEQUOIA NATIONAL PARK ★
CALIFORNIA

SAN DIEGO COUNTY

0   300 KM

Inset map

Kingcome
Knight Inlet
Homathko
Fraser
VANCOUVER ISLAND
MEMEKAY VALLEY
Squamish
BOWEN ISLAND
North Vancouver
Courtenay •
Vancouver
New Westminster
THETIS I.
Strait of Georgia
Abbotsford
• Hope
CARMANAH PACIFIC PROVINCIAL PARK
CARMANAH VALLEY ★
Chilliwack
Cheewhat Lake
Cowichan L.
WALBRAN VALLEY
Victoria •
OLYMPIC PENINSULA
Juan de Fuca Strait
Skagit
Admiralty Inlet
Forks •
OLYMPIC
Port Angeles •
Hoh
NATIONAL PARK
Port Discovery
Puget Sound
Kalaloch •
Quinault Lake
Port Orchard •
Seattle •
Cedar
Fort Lewis •
0   50 KM

IN MID-OCTOBER 1994 my husband and I came to an island in British Columbia to live, if not in a forest, at least with a forest at our backs. We had spent a quarter of a century on this coast and had visited the old-growth trees in Cathedral Grove on Vancouver Island and in Cypress Provincial Park high above the city of Vancouver. We had camped at Heart of the Hills on the Olympic Peninsula in Washington State and toured the redwood groves in northwestern California. I knew a western red cedar when I saw one, and like most people on the coast, I could spot a western hemlock from a distance by its weary uppermost tip. But about the species that grow to such colossal size here on the Pacific coast of North America I was colossally uninformed. As I did the research for this book, I also learned to identify the trees around me. I wanted to be able to recognize a Douglas fir at a distance by its shape or up close by its bark, needles, or cones. Initially the forest was chaotic – until I remembered Tosca's knife.

One Saturday afternoon when I was about 12 years old, I had, as usual, tuned my radio to the Metropolitan Opera broadcast as a background accompaniment to whatever else I was doing. But this day I paid attention while host Milton Cross described the second act of Tosca. He said listeners would hear Puccini's tormented heroine drop the knife with which she had just stabbed the evil Scarpia. That one detail dragged me out of indifference and admitted me to opera's previously impenetrable thickets, where I wander today, a self-taught enthusiast.

In the forest a Douglas fir seed cone became the equivalent of Tosca's knife. This unique cone, hanging from branches in such abundance, lying on the ground right under its parent tree, was something I could identify when the trees were indecipherable. With that one piece of information, all Douglas firs wore name tags and a portion of the forest was pinned down and could be studied with confidence. When eventually I knew Douglas firs in all their aspects, I moved on to the other species one by one, and soon the forest sorted itself out. Although I have gone walking in the woods with keys and charts, nothing worked as well for me as this in-depth species-by-species study.

This book is a portrait in words and photographs of 11 species that produce the largest of our coastal trees, with shorter essays on western yew, red alder, and madrone, or arbutus – three species interesting for reasons other than sheer size. I have included the giant sequoia, which does not grow on the coast, because it is linked by reputation with coast redwoods and because nothing else on earth achieves its mass. Although I write about individual giant trees and have created a combined American-Canadian list of the present champions, my focus is broader than that. I am portraying whole tribes of trees – where they live, how they reproduce, how they fit into forest ecosystems, how they differ from other trees, and what kind of wood they produce.

In the beginning I thought I would have to describe the giant species well enough so that a reader could confidently distinguish one from the other. Now, having read descriptions by many authors, I know that what they see isn't what I see. Dark green, I have discovered, is subjective, or a comparison – the needles of western hemlock being obviously dark green only next to the yellowish-green foliage of western red cedar. When Bob Herger began to show me his photographs of the trees, their leaves, and their cones, I tossed aside my concern about descriptions. His photographs may be all you need to identify many of the trees in this book, yet Bob has managed to capture not just the beauty and majesty of his subjects, but also their personalities. To look at his portraits is to know the trees.

Bob Herger and Washington's big-tree hunter Robert Van Pelt recognize trees with the same confidence the rest of us recognize our friends. In a fraction of a second we compute details, such as height, slope of the shoulders, and manner of walking, and we come up with Harry, even if it is dark and raining and Harry is half a block away. A tree is like that – the color of its leaves, the way it holds its branches, the structure of its bark, the size and placement of its cones or catkins – describable details but so minutely variable that seeing many individuals and getting to know a species intuitively is the only way. It is comfort to the confused to know that conifers are genetically complex, producing variations within species that affect, among other traits, their physical appearance. One day you just know a tree. Or you come pretty close to knowing. Donald Culross Peattie, author of dozens of books about nature, describes with precision and imagination the silva of western North America in *A Natural History of Western Trees,* but he warns that some trees, such as the several species of true fir, can be difficult to tell apart, and he offers this cheering advice: "Indeed no one need be ashamed of stating that he cannot name a given tree, of whatever sort, without waiting for the season to complete the flowering and fruiting of the annual life cycle."

When my husband and I bought our inaccessible slice of conifer-covered mountain slope, I thought of the trees as backdrop to a small rock plateau where our house sat. Fear of the forest blew in on the first windstorm, a not unusual reaction. I have heard of wives who have fled to the city with their children, refusing to return until the winter winds abate. I have heard of newcomers who clear away every single towering conifer before building their safe-as-the-suburbs houses. After a year, I knew more fully how dangerous the forest can be. One January night, when heavy snow was falling, I stood outside and shone a flashlight up into the Douglas firs and enjoyed a child-like moment of vertigo induced by descending snowflakes and sway-ing treetops. Minutes later I heard a branch crack somewhere. In a moment of confusion and fear I knew I was foolish to be out under those heavily burdened limbs. In that same storm our neighbor was walking from one house on her property to another when she heard a great tearing of branches, realized in a moment of terror that a tree was falling nearby, and had no time to flee before the thump of the trunk hitting the ground signaled that she was safe.

A year in the forest taught me to be cautious but conservative, in the true meaning of the word. I believe that *we* are what is out of place in this forest, and it is up to us to live here as considerately as possi-ble. We can do nothing about the trees that were cleared to build our house, but we can preserve the remaining ones, which means keep-ing them where we want them – standing upright and not lying down in our living room. We have felled only two precariously leaning trees of any size and, as I describe in the chapter on Douglas fir, have reduced the risk of being squashed by another.

Our Douglas firs, however, are individuals with a price on their heads. We may one day be all that stands between them and the saw, something we realized as we watched a man help himself to trees that had grown large and salable because of the forbearance of previ-ous owners over the past 100 years. Much of the steeply sloping hill behind and to the north of us has now been logged. For more than a month we endured the whine of the saw, the crack of severing trunks, and the heartbreaking groan every tree makes as it surrenders to gravity.

We can protect our two-and-a-half-acre forest by putting a con-servation covenant on the trees to prevent any future owner from log-ging. Since it is difficult to climb to the back of our property, I have no idea how many trees we own, but I find myself thinking about their future. Protecting them legally might make our land less attractive to buyers. Why should I do that? After studying the giant trees and their habits, I think I know why those trees should be preserved. They aren't magnificent old-growth, but they are vigorously growing, endlessly contributing to the health of this ecosystem that sustains me. My trees produce oxygen, absorb carbon dioxide, remove other pollutants from the air, enhance and stabilize the thin layer of soil on this rocky mountain, and feed the squirrels.

An acre of such trees will clean up the carbon dioxide I produce by driving my car 11,000 miles. Every day one of my trees supplies enough oxygen for four people. You may not feel the need to visit an oxygen bar because of them – certainly because of trees somewhere. If I am to go on using paper at the annual rate of North Americans, there has to be a tree growing somewhere for every year I am around. Symbolic though it may be, protecting some trees seems to be an obligation I owe the planet.

WHEN I STARTED TO RESEARCH this book, I was plagued by the idea that I was glorifying tree species whose giant manifestations had already vanished from the coast. At the time Europeans first arrived here the world's largest temperate rainforest ran from southeast Alaska through to northern California. It must have seemed as though those forests would never be depleted, and indeed logging went on and the forests went on throughout most of what the British Columbian author and academic Patricia Marchak calls "the profligate century." By the late 1980s it was clear that there could eventually be no more virgin forest to log. One estimate made in 1990 was that of the roughly 19 million acres of original old-growth forest in Oregon and Washington before European settlement, all of it would be gone by the year 2023, except for 1.17 million acres protected in national parks, wilderness areas, and research natural areas. (Much of the protected acreage is fragmented and at high elevations.) In the United States at that time, all the original old-growth forest on private lands had been cut, and the United States Department of Agriculture (USDA) Forest Service was allowing annual cuts of an estimated 31,000 acres of old-growth in nine national forests of Oregon and Washington.

In British Columbia the Sierra Club of Western Canada made exactly the same prediction about Vancouver Island, which in 1860 had had an estimated 5.6 million acres of ancient temperate rainforest. By 1990 2.04 million acres were left and, if recent annual cuts of 59,000 acres had continued, the forests would be gone by the year 2022. Although nine percent of the island had been protected in five major parks, the Sierra Club reported that much of that land was at high elevations or in bogs. It estimated that just 3.3 percent of the original rainforest had been protected and a large percentage of this was on steep slopes rather than in the low-elevation, flat terrain more typical of the original rainforests.

These are simply snapshots of the total picture of old-growth forests along this coast. And not pretty pictures at that. But in the last years of the 1980s – with the end of the rainforests predicted in our lifetimes – conservationists and environmentalists stepped up their efforts to preserve what was left. In 1991 American environmentalists won restrictions on logging to protect the northern spotted owl. President Bill Clinton held a Timber Summit in Oregon two years later and subsequently issued a plan to reduce timber cuts in the national forests to a quarter of what they had been in the 1980s. The USDA Forest Service announced a new mission – to keep ecosystems functioning, its old volume-based timber sales were to be replaced by calculations of what should be left behind to help troubled forests. Green consumers began to demand wood that had been taken from sustainably managed forests, with the help of certification agencies such as the Institute for Sustainable Forestry in Redway, California. The Public Forestry Foundation, a nonprofit organization that helps citizens influence the management of public forests, gave its approval to well-managed forests, such as the one on army land at Fort Lewis, Washington, and helped develop standards by which sustainable forestry operations could be judged and certified.

In British Columbia, following the 1993 summer of protests that saw 700 people arrested for blockading logging roads into Clayoquot Sound on Vancouver Island, a 19-member panel of scientists issued its report in 1995, recommending drastic changes to logging practices, including the limiting of clearcuts to 10 acres. The provincial government adopted every one of the panel's recommendations and announced the same year that it would move quickly to end conventional clearcut logging, to demand ecological assessments before allowing pristine watersheds to be logged, and to limit the percentage of road building in logging areas.

In 1996 the governing New Democratic Party added 24 small parks to the 120 it had created in the past five years. The new parks fulfilled the government's commitment to set aside 13 percent of Vancouver Island. By the year 2000 the government aims to have put 12 percent of the entire province in protected parks. Under the Forest Renewal Plan, logging companies pay higher stumpage fees, with the increased revenue going to retrain loggers, while the Forest Practices Code bans clearcut logging on unstable hillsides, in old-growth management areas, and beside streams in community watersheds.

Without being Pollyannaish, I see reason to hope that our attitudes to the coastal forests are changing. There is talk about focusing not on what we can take but on what we must leave behind. For inspiration we can look to an example such as Wildwood Tree Farm for a model of sustainable forestry. Merv Wilkinson's 136-acre Wildwood farm east of Ladysmith on Vancouver Island is a small operation, having provided only a third of Wilkinson's annual income, but it is a marvel of sustained forestry. Since 1945 Wilkinson (now in his eighties) has made cuts in his forest every five years and has removed more than the original estimate of 1.5 million board feet of standing timber, while restoring the forest to that original volume. His rule is never to cut more than the annual growth.

On a larger scale a good example of sustained forestry is the 50,000-acre military training forest at Fort Lewis, Washington, which the army gradually acquired between the mid-1930s and 1940 after it had been logged and was virtually without trees. Today the landscape is a mix of open prairie, oak woodlands, and forests dominated by Douglas fir but with some bigleaf maple, ponderosa pine, western red cedar, and western hemlock. Gary McCausland, who heads the forestry staff, believes in being less rather than more manipulative in the forest but does have his staff intervene in some ways, such as burning off Scotch broom and thinning out trees. "I'd like to see diversity in this stand," he said as we drove through a naturally regenerated area, "but why try to change what's natural?" Each year selective logging removes 10 million board feet from the forest, which is producing 37 million board feet a year, according to a Public Forestry Foundation audit. Douglas firs 120 feet high remain in a stand logged three times since 1972. "When I was going to school, we were always taught that Douglas fir has to be clearcut because you don't get any regeneration under standing trees," said McCausland. "But I look out there and see lots of Douglas fir."

The focus of this book is not forests but the species that grow to massive size here on the coast. Champion trees are exciting to visit, especially when they stand in old-growth forests, but these amazing indigenous species don't confine themselves to dense and distant forests. Nor are the champions always in remote locations. Canada's largest red alder and bigleaf maple are easily seen in Vancouver's Stanley Park, which has the last remnants of old-growth forest in the city. In fact, Canada's largest bitter cherry grows in Snug Cove on the island where I live. I spent a fine afternoon following a trail in the western part of Stanley Park, seeing spire-topped western red cedars and Douglas firs in the 230-foot range. Tree tours in the urban areas of southeastern Vancouver Island and the capital city of Victoria are outlined in *Trees of Greater Victoria,* published by the Heritage Tree Book Society of Victoria. With its help I enjoyed tracking down large Garry oaks and was surprised to find numerous giant sequoias.

Similarly Seattle has several parks with large trees: Seward Park has a forest preserve with centuries-old Douglas firs and western red cedars, and Schmitz Park in West Seattle has the only surviving old-growth forest in this urban area. I purchased a guidebook at the College of Forest Resources and followed the University of Washington's campus tree tour, which offered a rare chance to compare a coast redwood with a giant sequoia. (Smaller specimens of the two species are also growing near The Barn, a cafeteria on the campus of the University of British Columbia.) In Portland most of the giant species are well represented at the 175-acre Hoyt Arboretum. Even a dawn redwood, the Chinese native once thought to be extinct, grows here near a grove of 60-year-old coast redwoods and giant sequoias.

GIANT TREES ARE CHARISMATIC, awesome, easy to idolize. Forests are complex, made up of hidden and difficult-to-appreciate insects, fungi, and bacteria. It may be that only in old-growth forests, now mostly cut, were the trees given the chance to reach great age and size. It may be that second-growth forests will never be allowed to grow long enough to get to the point where the trees begin to put on those fabled girths and heights. But if we don't know the trees and appreciate their potential, we can't begin to understand and stand up for the kinds of forests they must have. In writing this book I have sought out a variety of people who for different reasons are enamored of our extraordinary giant tree species. I have talked to forest geneticists, forest ecologists, entomologists, foresters, park rangers, and big-tree hunters. In the people who use small quantities of wood to make fine objects – luthiers, bowyers, carvers, furniture makers – I found a reverence for the trees that supply their wood. I think of Isaac Tait, who carves western red cedar and red alder, never wastes wood, and tries in each of his works to convey his concern for vanishing old-growth forests. I think of Curtis Erpelding, who started making fine furniture from Douglas fir as a way of pointing out that we have been throwing this beautiful wood away on lesser uses. I think of Kevin Maher, who builds airplane wings of Sitka spruce, and who has planted a dozen spruce seedlings in a coastal clearcut to pay back what he has taken.

Reverence is inevitable when we look at the colossal trees with which we have been blessed. Graft onto reverence a personal mission to champion and cherish, and we may eventually deserve the trees we were given.

I NEVER EXPECTED to find a champion tree. Although I had been visiting big trees on my daily walks, I had only recently started to measure them. I realized that "big" and "really big" weren't adequate descriptions; the time had come for specifics. One afternoon in our island forest I guessed and then verified the girth of several large Douglas firs and western red cedars, wrapping my tape – as convention demands – at breast height above the bottom of the tree.

Girth counts the most in assessing the scores of champions. For its 56-year-old National Register of Big Trees, the citizens' conservation organization, American Forests, gives a point for each inch of circumference and a point for every foot of height, making circumference 12 times more important than height. This bias in favor of girth recognizes the growth pattern of most trees, which lengthen in youth and spread in maturity. American Forests also gives points for the size of the crown, which involves tracing its outline on the ground, measuring the widest and narrowest spreads, averaging the two, and awarding a point for every four feet.

For accurate height measurements, foresters use an Abney level, hypsometer (an instrument that estimates altitude), or a surveyor's transit. A favorite device of big-tree hunters is a handheld clinometer, which establishes the angle between ground level and an imaginary line running to the top of the tree. Using this angle and the distance from the tree, they are able to calculate the height.

The scores of champions within species are remarkably consistent: grand firs hit the 490s; yellow cedars and western hemlocks score around 530; Douglas firs rate in the high 700s; Sitka spruces climb to the low 900s; western red cedars ascend to the mid-900s; coast redwoods exceed 1,000 but not 1,100; and the giant sequoia stands on the ultimate plateau – an easy-to-remember 1,300 points for the largest tree in the world. General Sherman, as it is called, wins 998 points for circumference, 275 for height, and 27 for crown spread. It has been the national champion since 1940 when the register began.

When one considers only the species dealt with in this book, the three contiguous Pacific states share the national champions: Washington has the largest grand fir, Pacific silver fir, western hemlock (four individuals are national co-champions), Pacific yew, and a Sitka spruce that reigns with one in Oregon. That state also has the largest

9
—

With a footprint that would cover a house, 2,300-year-old General Sherman, in Sequoia National Park, is the world's largest living thing.

Douglas fir and bigleaf maple. California wins with a Pacific madrone (arbutus), Oregon white (Garry) oak, coast redwood, and the giant sequoia.

Some people – notably the rangers in California's Sequoia National Park where General Sherman resides – think the point system doesn't work for all trees; they measure the sequoias in their care according to the volume of wood they possess. Even by this standard, General Sherman is the biggest. With 52,508 cubic feet of wood – and at an estimated age of 2,300 to 2,700 years still adding 2,000 pounds a year – it beats out the General Grant and the Bull Buck trees, both of which have been nominated for its title. As a result of these challenges to the General's supremacy, American Forests has modified its system. It continues to use the point formula, but if a champion is challenged and the formula seems inadequate, accurate volume figures for both champion and challenger decide the issue.

ROBERT VAN PELT, the official big-tree coordinator of Washington State, knows what it is like to enter into one of these contests. Dr. Van Pelt is a dedicated giant hunter; his guide to the champions of Washington, published under the auspices of the College of Forest Resources at the University of Washington, records the biggest individuals of 728 species, many of which Van Pelt has tracked down himself. He and his wife, Kathy, the urban forester for the city of Tacoma, scour the state in their Toyota Previa, which has a license-plate frame reading TREE POLICE. To cover the vast unexplored areas of the state, they have perfected what they call 55-mile-an-hour dendrology – the knack of recognizing species at a distance from a moving car. Years of practice have made trees as easy to recognize as are their friends. "It's the gestalt of the tree," Van Pelt explains.

Tall, russet-bearded, and large of limb, Van Pelt has the gestalt of a red cedar. He is now in his mid-thirties and doing postdoctorate research at the University of Washington on the ecology of old-growth forests, specifically the response of understory plants to gaps in the canopy. Coming from Wisconsin to Washington in 1984, he found that the state had only 13 champion trees and no coordinator. He filled the vacant post and spurred the search, having now nominated 40 trees for the national list and giving the state 50 record holders.

Van Pelt says that most of the champion trees have been found because they are near trails and easily seen, but in 1992 he and a friend ventured for four days into the Olympic Mountains to remeasure an alpine fir. Having established a base camp a day's walk from the trailhead, they set off on what was supposed to be a short hike to their quarry. The pair found themselves in a fog-enshrouded, trackless

THE CHAMPS

	CIRCUMFERENCE	HEIGHT	CROWN SPREAD	POINTS	LOCATION
OREGON WHITE OAK (U.S. champ)	25'2"	122'	133'	457	El Dorado County, California
GRAND FIR (B.C. champ)	20'10"	234'	36'	493	Chilliwack River, B.C.
PACIFIC SILVER FIR (U.S. champ)	24'5"	217'	32'	518	Forks, Washington
BLACK COTTONWOOD (B.C. champ)	30'0"	142'	98'	527	Skumalasph Island, B.C.
WESTERN HEMLOCK (U.S. co-champ)	28'5"	174'	65'	531	Olympic National Park, Washington
BIGLEAF MAPLE (U.S. champ)	34'11"	101'	90'	543	Clatsop County, Oregon
YELLOW CEDAR (B.C. champ)	36'3"	203'	52'10"	651	Memekay Valley, B.C.
DOUGLAS FIR (U.S. champ)	36'6"	329'	60'	782	Coos County, Oregon
SITKA SPRUCE (U.S. co-champ)	58'11"	191'	96'	922	Olympic National Forest, Washington
WESTERN RED CEDAR (B.C. champ)	62'0"	194'	51'	951	Cheewhat Lake, B.C.
COAST REDWOOD (U.S. champ)	70'5"	313'	101'	1,183	Prairie Creek Redwoods State Park, California
GIANT SEQUOIA (U.S. champ)	83'2"	275'	107'	1,300	Sequoia National Park, California

wilderness where their maps were useless. After a night in the forest without tent or sleeping bag, they found their tree, which is a national champion. "It's on the edge of a grove and has branches all the way to the ground," Van Pelt told me. "It's in a beautiful part of the Olympics, about as far as you can get from any road."

Few people will ever see this fir, and that is just fine with Van Pelt, who is concerned about the effects of people hunting out trees in sensitive areas. That is why he likes an easy-to-view champion Sitka spruce at one end of an RV campground on the south shore of Quinault Lake on Washington's Olympic Peninsula. "I think of it as sort of a sacrificial tree, a token public tree. It's good to have a tree like that in a public place," he says.

The Quinault Lake spruce was also the focus of an interstate contest, which started when Van Pelt gave it 922 points. The longtime national champion Sitka spruce, with 902 points, was on the Oregon coast at Seaside. Twenty points isn't a significant spread when you are dealing with coastal conifers, and so on a December day when it poured rain, teams from Washington and Oregon traveled 500 miles to confirm the measurements. The problem, which was obvious when I visited the Quinault Lake spruce, was where to measure the circumference. At breast height there are huge buttressing roots that increase the girth considerably. After arguing about ground level, the state teams agreed to declare their entrants co-champions. (Normally, however, co-champs are within five points of one another.) It is because of problems like this that Van Pelt thinks the volume of a tree, especially of single-stem conifers, is a better indication of size.

The irony for Canadians in this saga of the spruces is that their poster-pinup Carmanah Giant is not the biggest Sitka spruce. With 703 points it trails its American cousins. But at 314 feet it *is* the tallest Sitka spruce on record. It is preserved today in Carmanah Pacific Provincial Park on the west coast of Vancouver Island. Among the species covered in this book, British Columbia has four trees that exceed the largest of their kind in the United States: based on points British Columbia has the largest black cottonwood, grand fir (a squeaker by two points), western red cedar, and yellow cedar.

Big-tree hunting is comparatively new to British Columbia. The province had an enthusiast in Randy Stoltmann, who published his *Hiking Guide to the Big Trees of Southwestern British Columbia* in 1987 and his *Guide to the Record Trees of British Columbia* in 1991. In May 1994, at the age of 30, Stoltmann died in a skiing accident in the Kitlope Valley. With the idea of continuing the register, forest ecologist Andy MacKinnon, with the B.C. Ministry of Forests, has tried but failed to find Stoltmann's records.

WHEN I SPOTTED an exceptionally large tree, I was driving through the village of Ridgefield in southern Washington. On the lawn of an old-fashioned, white-frame house on North Main Street, I identified a giant sequoia. It was a feat of 30-mile-an-hour dendrology.

The Hughes family were relaxing on their veranda in a cool breeze blowing from the Columbia River. They told me that a Lindley Meeker had planted three giant sequoias in Ridgefield, including the one in front of their house, which had been built in 1874. The tree had been struck by lightning and, in 1952, the top broke off in an ice storm, but it is still a graceful cone shape, fully branched, and growing vigorously. Townspeople once gathered around protectively when a man approached it with a chain saw, backing off when they learned he intended to trim only a few lower branches.

I was sure this individual was bigger than the champion of the species in Bob Van Pelt's registry. "Did you put a tape around it?" he asked when I visited him. I gave him the measurement. He did a quick calculation. I had already figured that the tree had to be only 85 feet tall to slay the current giant, and I was pretty sure it was over 100 feet. There was a pause. I imagined Van Pelt mentally felling the sequoia he had found in Mount Vernon. "It would be the largest," he said. "In fact, it would be the largest exotic tree growing in the state. If it checks out, I'll put your name in my next book."

A few months later I phoned him. "You're the lady who found the giant sequoia," he said. He told me the measurements: 32 feet, six inches in circumference, 125 feet tall, a 65-foot crown spread – for 531 points. "It's the new state champion," he said. I was absurdly pleased.

The Royal Couple Coast Redwood and Giant Sequoia

A MAN WALKING BY ME in a redwood grove in California said, "Makes you feel kind of small, doesn't it?" Was that true? I wondered. I felt elevated in those forests, not diminished. Perhaps one can feel smaller in a room whose shape and dimensions have been devised to deceive the eye. But the forest is not a fun house. It does not play tricks of perspective nor does it contain anything deviously incompatible in size. The cloverlike leaves of oxalis and the white berries of the fairy lantern in this grove beside Redwood Creek are in correct proportion to my hand as it reaches out to touch them. The sword ferns growing with them, although perhaps taller than I am used to, are in scale with the tan oak. Even the redwoods themselves seem proportionate on this rather small alluvial flat. I hug one of these trees – seven outstretched arm lengths and still I am short of my starting point. I calculate seven times my height plus a little more and figure that I am nose to bark with a trunk that is 41 feet in circumference, 13 feet in diameter. I raise my head until my neck aches, seeking the tops of trees that are two or three times as tall as the Douglas firs of my acquaintance. I cannot assimilate the outsized grandeur of these trees, which are the tallest in the world.

I have the same problem with the giant sequoia, the most massive of tree species. General Sherman, the world's *largest* living thing, has a diameter of 36.5 feet at its base and would completely cover the ground floor of my house, something I find hard to remember in the context of the Giant Forest, a plateau on the western slope of the Sierra Nevada, with its long open meadows and mountain panoramas. When an individual giant is not fenced off from tiny, admiring humans, as the General Sherman is, it is harder to comprehend its size. For instance, the Washington Tree, more than 30 feet in diameter and 250 feet tall, stands in a dense forest, a setting that moderates its mass so that it seems appropriate – a king among subjects.

Coast redwoods and giant sequoias, which are sometimes called Sierra redwoods, are members of the *Taxodiaceae* family, but each has its own genus and is the only species in that genus. The scientific binomial of coast redwoods is *Sequoia sempervirens*. The

Almost immune to fire and insect attack, giant sequoias, like this one in Grant Grove in California's Kings Canyon National Park, live until they become too large and fall over.

FOLLOWING PAGES
Giant sequoias grow in groves at high elevations on the west side of the Sierra Nevada, spending long winters draped in snow and surviving on only one inch of rain during the summer.

name *Sequoia*, suggested by the botanist Stephen Endlicher in 1840, recalls an Indian-European named Sequoyah, who invented a system of writing for the Cherokee language and taught thousands of his people to read and write. *Sempervirens* evokes the tree's evergreen and easy-sprouting habits.

The scientific naming of giant sequoia created an international fray in the mid-1850s when a British botanist suggested *Wellingtonia* as the genus name, and an American naturalist fired back the following year with *Washingtonia*. Bigtree, as it is sometimes called, had to wait until 1939 for its present binomial, *Sequoiadendron giganteum* – *dendron* being Greek for tree and *giganteum* for giant.

The two species are related to the swamp cypress or bald cypress of the southeastern states and to the dawn redwood, a deciduous evergreen thought to have been extinct but rediscovered in 1944 growing in the province of Szechwan in central China. White redwoods, found everywhere but the northern part of the redwood forests, are genetically abnormal shoots of normal coast redwoods.

Genetic studies confirm that the sequoias and the redwoods have been appropriately assigned to different genera. The coast redwood has 33 unpaired chromosomes to the giant sequoia's 11. Scientists have compared marker chromosomes in dawn redwoods and swamp cypresses and have concluded that they did not contribute to the redwoods. They have also decided that it is unlikely that coast redwood, with its complicated genetics, would have contributed to a less complex species like sequoia.

As much as 125 million years ago, ancestors of the three redwoods ranged over the northern hemisphere. Coast redwood fossils have been found in England and parts of western Europe, and dawn redwoods grew above the Arctic Circle. Coast redwoods and giant sequoias were in their present ranges 20 million years ago. Before the Sierra Nevada had risen very high, sequoias migrated from the eastern onto the western slopes, where the trees were gradually cut off as the mountains rose and the climate to the east became drier and hotter. Today giant sequoias are confined to 75 Sierra Nevada groves in central California, most of them southeast of Fresno, at an elevation of 4,590 to 6,560 feet. Of the 35,607 acres on which giant sequoias are found, only eight percent remain in private hands. National parks and forests, state and county parks, and Indian Bureau lands protect the remainder.

After the last Ice Age, the coast redwoods disappeared from the rest of the western United States and Canada but remained in a narrow 450-mile strip, 150 miles west of the sequoias, along the Pacific Ocean from central California to the extreme southwestern tip of

In Prairie Creek Redwoods State Park, Roosevelt elk browse in open meadows but use the humid, cool redwood forest for shelter and shade.

Oregon. The coast redwoods were seen by European explorers who stepped ashore on the north coast of California in the 1770s, by overland explorer Jedediah Smith in 1828, and by gold-seeking adventurers in 1849. When gold fever abated, redwood fever took hold and logging began. Alarmed conservationists formed the Save-the-Redwoods League in 1918 and immediately bought redwood forest land, which provided the basis for three state parks. In the 1960s the National Park Service determined that of the original 2,000,000 acres of virgin redwood forests, only 300,000 remained uncut, and only 50,000 were protected in state parks.

One result was the creation in 1968, and the augmentation a decade later, of Redwood National Park, which includes within its boundaries the three state parks created in the 1920s. About half of the remaining old-growth acreage is in this cooperatively managed national and state preserve. Farther south, Humboldt Redwoods State Park has a large component of old-growth. The Save-the-Redwoods League has purchased more than 80,000 acres of ancient redwoods, which are protected in Redwood National Park, Humboldt Redwoods State Park, and other smaller parks and preserves. When some groves in private hands were included, it was estimated in 1990 that 98,500 acres of old-growth remained in the state. Another 140,100 acres of young redwood forest are in public parks and reserves.

About a third of the virgin giant sequoia acreage was logged, with entire groves disappearing, before a halt was called to the slaughter. The authors of a publication produced by the Sequoia Natural History Association describe logging operations in which shattered trees were left on the ground or unmanageable trunks were dynamited into useless fragments. "The devastation and squandering in sequoia logging was beyond belief," they write. "Healing will take centuries; the shambles remaining are perhaps the greatest monument to man's destructive lumbering enterprises in this country."

EVEN THOUGH they are genetically distinct and geographically separated, the two California giants are often grouped together because of the characteristics they share. They both have red heartwood, which because of its tannins resists decay. The sapwood of a downed giant sequoia will rot away, while heartwood lying on the ground has been known to be well preserved after two centuries. Neither tree exhibits typical signs of aging. Sequoias, for instance, can still produce cones when they are 3,000 years old and continue to amass wood century after century. The two species share great size and age but with slight differences: the redwoods grow taller, averaging 300 feet; the sequoias average 250 feet but are more massive, with average breast-height diameters in the six-foot range and large trees measuring 25 to 30 feet across. The oldest known redwood reached 2,200 years, while the average member of the species in a virgin forest lives to be 500 to 700; the oldest known sequoia was 3,200 and the present largest specimen – the General Sherman – is estimated to be 2,300 to 2,700.

Generally sequoias and redwoods are encircled by shallow roots, which extend four to six feet down and 125 feet out from the tree. Redwoods have no taproot; sequoias draw on taproots and lateral roots until the tree is six to eight years old, when the taproot ceases to elongate. In one study researchers dug a trench along a sequoia root, following it from the tree where it was four feet underground. Slanting upward, the root ended 125 feet out and a foot below ground level. In another experiment, marked water put into one redwood was detected in another 500 feet away, showing that the roots were connected.

Both trees usually live until they fall over. Protected by their thick, resin-free barks, older redwoods and sequoias survive ground fires, although they bear the scars of many. Redwoods survive with large burned-out areas at their bases. Known as goose pens, these cavities were used by pioneers as cages for domestic fowl. Neither tree is killed by disease, but both can be attacked by fungi, which will rot wood and roots. For a variety of reasons – root rot, fire scars at ground level, uneven weights of snow on the branches – old trees become unbalanced and topple. Sometimes they come down like dominos. In March 1991 a very old redwood fell in Humboldt State Park, hitting a 1,000-year-old tree, which leaned but didn't succumb. A week later the leaner fell, bringing with it the Dyerville Giant, which had been the champion coast redwood since 1966.

WHILE THE TWO TREES ARE SIMILAR, they are perhaps more interesting in their distinctions – in the way they respond to their very different habitats and in their reproductive and regenerative mechanisms. Entering a coast redwood forest is somewhat like stepping into an air-conditioned building from enervating heat, except that the forest is moderately cool, humid, and energizing. Fog phantoms steal off the ocean and into the redwoods, hanging about in the upper canopy, and through that misty atmosphere come shafts of sunlight to warm you on the forest floor, where you luxuriate in oxygen-rich air. In utter contrast the sequoias live in sharp heat and thin, dry air in the summer. Even early in the morning, photographer Bob

21

COAST REDWOOD
AND GIANT SEQUOIA

Herger found the light harsh and intense – like being under a magnifying glass, he said.

Coast redwoods survive best in a humid habitat that they help to create through transpiration. Large trees may release as much as 500 gallons of water a day from their needles. When this moist envelope meets a cool ocean fog, water condenses onto the leaves and drips from the canopy, creating a life-sustaining soft rain to replace soil water. Fog-bathed upper branches remain green, but often the tops of trees that have emerged above the general crowd into the summer sun will die of desiccation.

Giant sequoias, on the other hand, spend their summers in dryness and bright sunlight and their winters draped in snow. For eight months of the year they receive moisture in the form of snowfalls; sometimes a snow pack of six feet builds up on their trunks. In the summer months, when thunderstorms are more likely than misty showers, they usually make do with an inch of rain.

Coast redwoods, as you might guess, are highly tolerant of shade. They can photosynthesize in low light and will grow in 10 percent of full sunlight. To make the greatest use of light and to minimize the loss of water, they have two kinds, or shapes, of leaves. On the shaded lower branches of the canopy, the leaves are like fir needles – hard, flat, splayed to receive as much light as possible, and waxy to reduce water loss. The upper branches bear scalelike leaves, resembling those of a juniper or cypress, that resist drying in wind and sun. The giant sequoia's single type of leaf is similar to the high-canopy leaves of the redwood.

While giant sequoias aren't known to grow from sprouts, coast redwoods do. The tourist industry exploits this phenomenon. In gift shops, convenience stores, and gas stations along the Redwood Highway, water-filled plastic tubs hold knobs of redwood burl, sporting soft, feathery shoots resembling springtime asparagus. Burls are those warty-looking protuberances on the boles of redwoods, which can weigh hundreds of pounds. They are often carved into ungainly bears and Indian heads by chain-saw-wielding craftsmen at events such as the Orick Burl Wood Fest.

In nature a burl seems to be a backstop, remaining dormant unless the tree is injured, at which point hormones trigger the sprouting of buds, which resemble potato eyes. Similarly, if a crown dies or is damaged, buds along the trunk will produce an array of soft foliage, which will eventually become a normal but narrow crown. Locally these trees are called fire columns. The most successful sprouts spring from root crowns of older trees or from dormant buds at the base of the logged stumps. They are linked to the

Before the Sierra Nevada reached its present height, giant sequoias migrated from the eastern to the western slopes, where they are now found in 75 distinct groves.

parent tree's root system but soon develop their own roots and form a circle – a fairy ring – around their common parent. As many as 100 sprouts have been found circling a stump, and it seems that the more sprouts there are, the better they all grow. Even seedlings have the ability to sprout from a collar of buds at their base. A young seedling, eaten by a browsing elk, will sprout again and again from these buds. Perhaps because they draw on a parent's root system, sprouts grow faster than seedlings. Twenty-year-olds have reached heights of 50 feet.

On my way to revisit the redwoods, I stopped off at the College of Forest Resources on the campus of the University of Washington in Seattle. On the lower branches of an evergreen near Anderson Hall, I recognized the olive-shaped cones of a coast redwood, which have scales resembling human lips. The female cones of the coast redwood, which are green at first, become reddish-brown and eventually weather to gray. The seeds they carry – about 60 to a cone – ripen a year after pollination and are released when the cones have dried. Because redwood forests are usually damp when the seeds are ripe, it may take several months before the seed falls out. On the other hand, it is thought that rain may help release the seeds by dissolving tannic crystals in the cone.

The University of Washington coast redwood has a giant sequoia neighbor. I wasn't surprised by the absence of cones on that tree, or on the ground around it, because sequoias tend to hang on to their cones for many years, and most of the cone crop is found in the upper parts of the crown. While the giant sequoia seed cone resembles the redwood cone, with the same lip-shaped scales, it takes two years to ripen and becomes as large as a chicken egg. In the first year it produces chlorophyll, which causes it to be green. The number of scales is hereditary, usually 25 to 40, but some researchers have counted 56. Each scale has four to seven seeds, and it is estimated that an average cone has 200. The cones can stay unopened on the tree for up to 20 years. While a mature tree – beginning about age 150 to 200 and continuing into old age – may produce 1,500 cones a year, as many as 10,000 to 30,000 may adorn a single tree. The green cones continue to photosynthesize: their peduncles – or stems – have annual growth rings that can be counted to determine their age. Because cones are held for a long time, scientists wondered why their seeds do not germinate inside the cone. The answer seems to be a tannin-containing liquid, known as red cone pigment, which inhibits germination (it also makes a nonfading ink for writing).

In fact, one of the marvels of giant sequoia reproduction is the

Tall Tree, measured in 1963 at 367.8 feet in height, rises above its companions and dwarfs a human visitor to this protected grove of coast redwoods on an alluvial flat of Redwood Creek.

process of releasing and distributing seed. Visitors who come to the sequoia groves after spending some time in the muffled hush of the redwoods may be surprised by the noise – the hammering of woodpeckers and a strange chattering or high-pitched call from the trees above. Soon a furry-tailed fellow appears, descending the bole like an employee on a mission for the boss, except that this little worker is self-employed, the proprietor of this particular tree and some acres around it. The chickaree, or Douglas squirrel, is a territorial mammal, active year-round gathering food from the trees it has staked out and then protects from invaders by being vocally aggressive. It likes to eat the fleshy green scales of young cones, but not the seeds, which are too small and lack nutrition. When there are lots of chickarees around, the animals cut down large numbers of cones and carry them to a safe cache where they later eat them, scattering seeds, which may germinate in time. When competition is reduced, chickarees will eat what comes to paw in the upper branches, sending the seeds winging down and helping to disperse them over a wider area.

Fire plays such an important role in the ecology of the sequoia forest that scientists have decided the trees would likely not exist without it (see "Foes and Friends," page 63). Fire helps to dry out cones, releasing the seed. It prepares a good seedbed by burning off organic matter and leafy plants, creating spaces in the mineral soil into which seeds can fall. To germinate and survive as a seedling, sequoia seeds need to hit an ecological jackpot. A seed that lands on mineral soil will do better than one that puts its roots down through litter. A seed embedded about three-eighths of an inch in moist soil will do better than one on a surface that dries out or one sunk so deeply into a crevice that its shoot can't reach up into the light. A seed developing in half-sunlight will do better than one in deep shade. Getting started under a blanket of snow seems to give a seedling a good whack at survival. By the time the snow melts, the seedling will have two-inch-long roots to supply moisture to fledgling leaves.

Light fires that don't destroy the canopy have been shown to stimulate the regeneration of the giant sequoias by controlling white firs and incense cedars. They are also useful in burning off accumulated vegetation that might feed a huge fire. Researchers tallying the size and frequency of fire in sequoia groves in the past 2,000 years have found that long intervals between conflagrations led to more intense and widespread fires. Frequent small fires, in effect, prevented catastrophic ones. After a period of official suppression, fires have been gradually reintroduced as a forest-management tool both in the prairies of the redwood forests and in the sequoia groves. Since the late 1960s the park service has deliberately set carefully planned late-spring and early-fall blazes, hot enough to burn off competing vegetation but controlled so that they won't damage the sequoias. In Redwood National Park fire is used to control Douglas fir, which encroaches on oak woodlands.

A century ago the loggers who attacked the sequoia forests with their rapacious saws discovered and ignored a frailty of the giant trees: when felled they shatter. The even-grained wood of the sequoia is brittle and has a low tensile strength. Sometimes as much as three-quarters of the wood of a giant tree would be wasted, left to be a fire hazard in the forest or taken away to become fence posts and pencils.

The wood of coast redwoods is beautiful, varying in color from the creamy sapwood to the auburn heartwood. It has unique cells, which are thin-walled, open, and much longer than wide. It has large fibers and little or no pitch or resin. As a result, redwood is lightweight but comparatively strong; it is easy to work, takes any finish applied to it, and glues readily. It is also resistant to fire and chemicals; insulates well against heat, cold, and sound; and imparts no taste or odor. Architects love it for the interior and exterior of buildings (mansions entirely of redwood were once proudly built); winemakers in California and France have preferred it for vats; it has found its way into coffins, bleachers, shingles, chimney pipes, outdoor furniture, hot tubs, cigar boxes – the list goes on.

And so it seems will California's state trees. According to the California Redwood Association, young redwood forests on private land are growing quickly and "forest industry experts expect to double the rate of timber growth on their lands by the year 2040." In 1994 young-growth trees were supplying 60 percent of the log production.

AS THE CALIFORNIA REDWOOD ASSOCIATION points out, the best groves of redwoods are at the mouths of rivers and on river benches, and these groves have been preserved. Tall Trees Grove is in Redwood National Park between Orick and Trinidad. Thirty cars a day and a shuttle bus are allowed to drive the six-mile gravel road to the head of a foot trail, which winds down through a mixed forest of Douglas firs, tan oaks, grand firs, and redwoods to the magical grove on the alluvial flats beside Redwood Creek. In 1963 when the area was surveyed by the National Park Service – with a $64,000 grant from *National Geographic* – to find the remaining old-growth forests and to determine the best place for a park, trees here were accurately measured and found to be the three tallest in the world. The following year, and twice in the 1970s, Redwood Creek flooded, depositing sand, silt, and clay around the trees. Tall Tree, which in 1963 was measured at 367.8 feet, in 1995 was found to have a dead top and seven feet of soil built up around its base, in effect reducing its height. A second living stem is catching up to the dead one, but Tall Tree has been pushed off the summit by the *National Geographic* Tree, which in 1963 was the third-tallest. On March 25, 1995, it was measured by two people. One declared the world's tallest tree to be 365.5 feet; the other made it 366 feet.

Looking up into the crown as I stand beside the widowmakers – two limbs that have fallen so far and fast they are embedded almost vertically in the forest floor – I realize I am like a football fan at one end of the field watching a match that is taking place exclusively at the other end. I try to get into the game by entering the space between two trees whose distant branches touch. In the enclosure formed by their trunks, the sounds of the forest and the voices of people are muffled. I think of the interlocked network of roots seeking underground and imagine a column of water in the cells, unbroken from probing root tips to laboring, breathing stomata (through which gases are exchanged with the atmosphere) – 500 gallons a day drawn endlessly. Above, the sun is shining on enchantingly pale green leaves, where the photosynthetic action happens. A little wind stirs the narrow crowns and I watch something spin down and down. Like a pass receiver, I snaffle the missile and accept the canopy's gift – a tiny section of twig and awl-like leaves.

Hoping that distance would put the trees into perspective, I cross Redwood Creek and look back at Tall Tree, rising above the alders and shorter redwoods. Only when a man steps out of the forest on the riverbank opposite do I understand *how* tall that tree is. At home I make a reminder. I put a sticker at the top of my office door and label it Tall Tree. At the bottom of the door I tape a representation of a human being – a wooden matchstick shortened to one and a quarter inches. The scale is mathematically accurate, but the difference is impossible. Isn't it?

Now, if Uncle Wiggily and all his little friends came out and nibbled on the spruce branches in 1752, we'll tell you how the dendrochronologist knows the sunspots were flaring that year. . . .

IF YOU ARE OF A CERTAIN AGE, you might recall Uncle Wiggily as the rabbit hero of a longtime series of newspaper bedtime stories for children, which always ended with a similar enigmatic teaser. In this case Uncle Wiggily is the snowshoe hare of northern Canada and Alaska, and the story is a scientific one read from tree rings by Anthony Sinclair and his colleagues in the Zoology Department of the University of British Columbia. It is just one example of the way dendrochronology reads history from tree rings.

Before following the trail of the snowshoe hare, it is useful to understand how trees grow and form their annual rings. Unlike a human child, who lengthens all over, trees grow taller only at the top; but like adult persons, trees put on girth. This outward (or radial) growth takes place in twigs, branches, trunk, and roots, and is created in a layer known as the cambium.

The cambium can be seen immediately under the bark as a moist, perhaps sticky, film. It is the only part of the trunk that grows – a layer the thickness of a single cell. It is constantly dividing to produce new cells on its outer and inner surfaces. The outer cells form the phloem (or inner bark), which carries nutrients down from the leaves to the branches, trunk, and roots. As new cells are added to the inner surface of the phloem, the cells on its outer surface die and become bark. On the inner side of the cambium, cells are created and added to a wider layer called the xylem (or sapwood), which carries water and nutrients to the leaves. Since more wood than bark is produced, the cambium makes four or five xylem cells for each phloem cell.

Across its width and nearing the middle of the tree, the xylem is gradually becoming more and more woody as its aging cells dry up. Xylem fades into heartwood, which is no longer living but serves to support the tree. And so we have the layers of a tree: bark, phloem, cambium, xylem, heartwood, and – at the very center – pith, which may decay or burn out, leaving the tree hollow at its core but still standing and thriving.

In each growing season the cambium contributes two shapes of cells to the xylem. The cells of spring are lighter-colored, thinner-walled, and of a larger diameter than the summer ones. The result in the wood is a light-colored band, known as earlywood, and a darker band, known as latewood. Latewood is stronger than earlywood, which was produced faster. Together the two form one annual ring. Scientists – dendrochronologists or dendroclimatologists – read the rings of harvested trees, of standing stumps, and of living trees. To sample a living tree, a scientist uses a hollow auger, which removes a pencilwide core.

Perhaps the most familiar use of tree rings are dated cross sections on display in ecology centers or museums. Counting back from the year the trees were cut, someone has established when they started growing and has flagged the significant events in human history during which they lived. Such a display is a potent reminder of the comparative brevity of human life and of human civilizations. If we could auger slowly through to the core of the General Sherman – the sequoia that is the world's largest living thing – we would be in touch with every year of history back to the birth of Jesus and still have another 300 to 700 years to go.

But in all truth, flagged cross sections are a human-centered way of looking at chronological events. A tree writes its own life story in its rings. We can tell, for instance, that a tree had been working hard to regain and retain an upright position. Softwoods and hardwoods do this by forming more wood on one side of the tree. The annual rings of a leaning conifer will be wider on the down side because the tree has attempted to push itself up. Hardwoods do the opposite: they attempt to *pull* themselves up by forming harder wood with larger rings on the top side of a leaning stem.

A poignant example of a tree's struggle to survive was read by Emanuel Fritz, a professor of forestry at the University of California at Berkeley, who examined a coast redwood that fell on March 13, 1933. The tree had sprouted about the year 700 A.D. Seven floods gradually buried its base to a depth of 11 feet so that the section of stump examined by Professor Fritz had rings going back only to 728. In 1147 the south side of the tree was injured in a fire. It healed itself, but because it was weakened, the redwood developed ring shake – a fissure along the annual ring caused by shaking – and rot crept into the wood. Still the tree grew. In 1595 another fire injured the north side of the tree, leaving five scars. Fires, in 1789 and 1806, attacked again on the north, and the tree began to form a buttress to counter a developing tilt. In 1820 a severe fire killed almost half the north side, burning off bark, sapwood, and some heartwood. In an effort to support itself on this injured side, the redwood produced an enormous buttress, which grew for more than a century, adding half an inch a year. On the day of its death, heavy rains had softened the ground and the buttress was unable to keep the 500 tons of wood from crashing down.

The Laboratory of Tree-Ring Research at the University of Arizona is now the center for North American studies in dendrochronology and dendroclimatology. Scientists here are using tree-ring data to investigate the effects of long-past natural and human disturbances on forest ecosystems. From tree rings they can observe signs of unusual climatic cooling and relate them to major volcanic eruptions. They also address our current concerns about rising carbon dioxide levels, acid rain, and environmental pollution.

Back in the boreal forest, what do tree rings tell us about Uncle Wiggily? When a hare nibbles at a spruce sapling, a scar forms on the annual rings. Assuming that more scars meant a larger number of nibbling rabbits, the University of British Columbia researchers constructed a profile of the snowshoe hare population in a single Yukon forest. They were able to trace a pattern of highs and lows going back 250 years. These recurring 10-year cycles closely track the 10.6-year cycles of intense and low sunspot activity. The link is not simple, but it is, according to Dr. Sinclair, the first one found between sunspots and animals.

And the record was written in the trees.

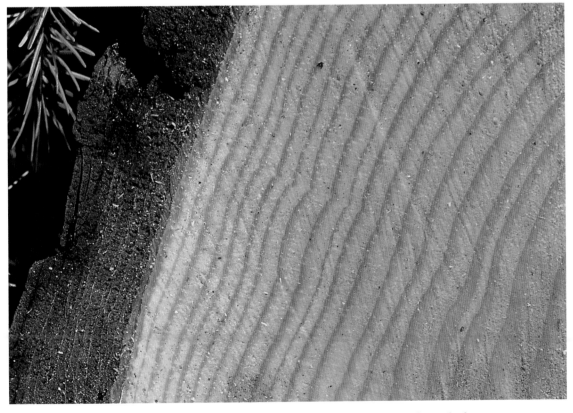

A wet spring, a hot summer, a distant volcanic eruption – the annual rings of a Douglas fir tell its life story and record our climatic history.

The Timber Titan Douglas Fir

It is January. The Douglas firs I can see from every window of my island home are in a pregnant winter pause. I have been watching them closely for a year now, ever since we hired an arborist to trim the sail on the one that seemed most likely to crash down on our house or drop its branches on our heads when the Squamish wind gusts from the north. Before he hitched himself up its 30-inch-wide bole in his cleated boots and safety harness, Ian Woodward said the big fellows around us had likely been growing since the island was logged a century ago, and he estimated they were 100 feet tall. It took Ian about an hour to trim away the dead branches and some of the living ones, leaving a barbered but more wind-resistant tree. Neighbors have since told me about a Douglas fir that came down in a windstorm here a few years ago. Its roots lifted a house and left it at a 30-degree tilt. I keep in mind the species' tendency to keel over in a high wind and examine our nearest mighty neighbors for any sign that their hold on the earth might be loosening.

Not a true fir but a member of a distinct genus, coastal Douglas firs range from central British Columbia to California. Near Hope, British Columbia, Douglas firs mingle with bigleaf maples.

Throughout this year in the forest I have learned to see our Douglas firs both as individuals and as examples of the form the tree takes as it ages. I came to the forest with a city-dweller's preference for tidy, well-shaped vegetation, and the irregularity of the forest – tipsy trees growing at odd angles and fallen ones lying helter-skelter – offended my eye. I was particularly upset by a downed log near the compost pit, until one day, as I was depositing our vegetable parings, I noticed a seedling on the log. Douglas firs prefer to germinate in mineral soil and are not usually found on nurse logs, but the pointed buds at the ends of the tiny branches and the pointed, but not sharp, needles surrounding the branch like a bottlebrush identified the seedling as an infant of the species. Now I see that it has two distinct whorls of branches, indicating two years' growth, and a healthy leader, which has risen above the curve of the nurse log into the sunlight, which Douglas fir seedlings demand. I am doubtful of the seedling's chance: Douglas firs need to be rooted in soil where they enter into a symbiotic relationship with fungi that help them take in mineral nutrients and water. Our littlest Douglas fir will likely succumb to drought.

On the sunny, oceanside of our property, a youngish Douglas fir, round in shape, light green, and as huggable as a child, has chosen a spot that will inevitably create a problem for us. It is on the shady edge of a grove of arbutus and juvenile Douglas firs established in a soil-filled declivity on the rocky slope that falls away from our house. A wooden staircase takes us to the shelf in the rock where these trees are growing, and the upstart Douglas fir will eventually block our path. As pretty as it is, I see that it is deformed. It has two leaders – a not uncommon characteristic of Douglas firs, and a habit with this one. Twice before, a twinned leader has formed, with one becoming an upward-reaching branch, unbalancing the symmetry of the little tree.

Nearby is a Douglas fir without a leader – it looks like a stalk of broccoli, or like the famous Cauliflower Tree, an unusual 160-year-old Douglas fir that was still growing in 1980 on private property between Invermere and Golden, British Columbia. Most of the juveniles on the sunny slope in front of our house are straight and well shaped, with annual whorls of branches spaced out along their trunks. They are still young enough to have smooth gray bark with resin-filled blisters like those on real firs, which I pop open for the pleasant smell. Their needles have an apple or balsam aroma when lightly crushed; they were used by First Nations peoples to make a coffeelike drink. If I look closely, I see that they are grooved down the center of their top sides, and underneath there are whitish rows – formed by the stomata – through which gases are exchanged with the atmosphere. The branches near the tops of these trees angle upward, but lower down the main branches flatten out and are nearly horizontal, although, like a rising inflection at the end of a sentence, their outer ends point upward. The distance between the whorls often exceeds two feet, and projecting that annual growth onto the tree, I imagine them a decade from now shutting me back into the forest like Sleeping Beauty.

Behind, on a forested slope, are mature Douglas firs that have acquired a coat of corky, furrowed bark, which on a cut log looks like bacon. Very old trees, with bark that can be 12 inches thick, are well protected in a forest fire. My trees have lost their lower branches and the living crown covers only the upper third of their boles. Yet they still have growing leaders and retain the familiar Christmas-tree shape. In time they will become like the aged ones near the ocean, whose limbs have been amputated by wind and abrasion and whose broken, flattened tops invite watchman eagles.

IN ITS ABILITY TO GROW TALL, Douglas fir reigns with the sequoias and redwoods. On good sites it can add three feet a year. The tallest tree in the world today is a coast redwood that measures 366 feet. Douglas firs have exceeded that height. Al Carder in *Forest Giants of the World Past and Present* cites two Washington State individuals measured in 1924 and 1933: the Nisqually Tree was 380 feet; the Mineral Douglas fir was 393 feet. In British Columbia Douglas firs over 350 feet were numerous in the sheltered habitat of Lynn Valley, now part of the municipality of North Vancouver. Both Dr. Carder and the late Randy Stoltmann, in his *Guide to the Record Trees of British Columbia*, report that Alfred John Nye, who was the first person to preempt land in the valley, felled a 415-foot behemoth there in 1902. Today's tallest, at 329 feet, is in Oregon, the state that has chosen the Douglas fir as its arboreal emblem.

Out of the ancient forest in British Columbia's Lynn Valley came the legend of the Cary Fir, a tale so enduring that it was recently repeated (although transposed to Vancouver Island) in an issue of *Taunton's Fine Woodworking*. The story was that in 1895 a Lynn Valley logger named George Cary cut down a Douglas fir measuring 417 feet in length and 25 feet through the stump. In 1922 the *Western Lumberman* ran a cover photograph of a dozen people and a dog posed on this famous tree, beginning the controversy over the authenticity of both the tree and the photograph. Doubters said that either the photograph had been faked with superimposed human figures (an unlikely technical accomplishment at that time) or the tree was a redwood. Even in 1979 silviculturists and foresters were split on this issue, with some declaring it a coast redwood and others a Douglas fir. In a recent issue of its newsletter, the Forest History Association of British Columbia presented the facts and concluded that the photograph was genuine but that the super-large Douglas fir in Lynn Valley – the so-called Cary Fir – never existed. The photograph, it declares, was likely taken in Vancouver's Kerrisdale area where crowds of people came to see an enormous Douglas fir cut down in 1896. The Kerrisdale tree was genuine: it was received at the city's Hastings Mill where the superintendent of timber operations reported it to be 400 feet long and 13 feet, eight inches in diameter, proving again that the tallest Douglas firs once surpassed today's tallest coast redwood.

From pollen studies we know that Douglas firs appeared in the Pacific Northwest 8,000 years ago. By the time Europeans arrived, the species had established the longest latitudinal range of any conifer of western North America. From the head of the Skeena River in northern British Columbia, a coast variety grows south to the mid-California coast, while the Rocky Mountain variety continues all the way into the mountains of central Mexico. The inland

variety can become big, but it is a slower-growing, shorter-lived tree with leaves that are bluish-green.

Disturbed only by fire and windstorms, coastal Douglas firs typically lived for about 750 years, but some were more than a millennium old when they were cut down. In his list of verified ancient trees of British Columbia, Randy Stoltmann includes a Douglas fir that grew on Waterloo Mountain on Vancouver Island: a ring count put its age at 1,307. Dr. Carder writes of a 1,266-year-old Vancouver Island tree and a Washington State tree that had 1,400 annual rings.

Even today when people on the coast talk about fir, this is the tree they mean. They also call it red fir, Oregon pine, Douglas tree, or Douglas spruce. Early taxonomists mirrored the public confusion by classifying the tree as a pine, fir, and hemlock before coming to the conclusion that it belonged to a rare genus, the members of which grow only in western North America and eastern Asia. In 1867 a new name – *Pseudotsuga* – was chosen. In his two-volume *Manual of the Trees of North America*, first published in 1905, Charles Sprague Sargent called it "a barbarous combination of a Greek with a Japanese word," and it does seem slanderous to have labeled our fine Douglas firs as "false hemlocks."

The Latin name of the species is *Pseudotsuga menziesii*. Its common name – Douglas fir – acknowledges the botanist David Douglas. However, despite its name, the Douglas fir is not a true fir. And why not? For one, because its seed cones hang down. Unless you are a bird or a canopy researcher, you will have a problem getting close to true-fir cones. They perch upright on the uppermost branches and, in the fall, they break up scale by scale on the tree. In contrast Douglas fir seed cones hang from branches and remain intact, decorating the tree like Christmas ornaments or littering the ground around it when they eventually fall off. Walk with your head down if you want to find a Douglas fir among very tall trees. The spent cones, reddish-brown and three inches long, are unmistakable: each scale is overlapped by a unique three-pronged bract, which protrudes like a naughty child's tongue and looks like Poseidon's magic trident.

The shapes of the needles and buds also separate *Pseudotsuga* from the true fir *Abies*. Douglas fir needles have pointed tips (but are not sharp like a spruce) while the ends of fir needles are rounded and indented at the center, like the top of a valentine. Douglas fir buds, at the ends and on the sides of branchlets, are pointed, which is rare among conifers, while fir buds have a more usual rounded shape.

Genetic work on Douglas fir began as early as 1912 in Washington and Oregon. Inbreeding and crossbreeding started in British Columbia in the mid-1950s. Jack Woods is a research geneticist with

OPPOSITE

Douglas fir needles are pointed but not sharp and are arranged in a spiral around the twig. Also pointed, the shiny brown buds at the ends of twigs are a good clue to identifying the species.

PREVIOUS PAGES

Pollen records show that Douglas firs have been in the Pacific Northwest for 8,000 years. Some individuals survived for more than 1,300 years and reached heights greater than those of today's tallest redwoods.

the B.C. Ministry of Forests. His work involves understanding the genetic patterns of conifers and, because of its commercial value, Douglas fir is a focus for him. "Conifers," he says, "are the most diverse organisms on the planet. Using biochemical measures, conifers are two and a half times more diverse than human beings. The reason we see the diversity in people and not in trees is because we don't look at trees closely. The tendency has been to associate all differences in conifers with the environment in which the tree grows. The more I work with Douglas fir, the more I attribute differences to genetics. Everything is under genetic control – growth rate, crown shape, wood density."

Today the search for genetically superior trees focuses on stem volume, wood density, and stem form. One problem that creates a defect in the wood begins when young trees flush twice in a growing season, producing a second leader. If one leader becomes a branch, it will grow up at a steep angle, creating a long knot that persists as the tree puts on wood. Ramicorn branching, as it is called, is associated with lammas growth, or second flushing, which tends to happen in juvenile trees growing on rich sites and is a characteristic under genetic control. Another wood-damaging trait under genetic control is stem sinuosity – long leaders that twist and, as a result, produce wood that is twisted.

In the Skagit River valley mighty Douglas firs associate with flamboyant Pacific rhododendrons.

COMMERCIAL LOGGING of the Pacific slope forests began in 1828. Dr. John McLoughlin, the Quebec-born "Father of Oregon" and superintendent of the Hudson's Bay Company's Columbia District, built a mill and started cutting Douglas fir at Fort Vancouver, 100 miles up the Columbia River. The first loggers of the 1800s, attacking these immense trees with their puny axes, were unprepared for the result. A man named Clem Bradbury, working near the river, is said to have cut into the sapwood of a Douglas fir and unleashed a fountain of pitch that poured out of the tree until the following morning. When he could resume work, he chopped for six hours before bringing the tree down. The superiority of the wood was apparent. Some fine straight boles of Douglas fir were selected for special purposes – in the 1860s one was erected in London's Kew Gardens as a flagpole and others became masts for ships of Britain's Royal Navy.

In the past century of intense logging, Douglas fir has been described as the greatest lumber source the world has ever known. Its strong, stiff, and durable wood is used as structural timber by engineers and builders; as framing lumber in light and heavy construction; for pilings, railway ties, and concrete forms; for tanks and vats, plywood and paper, window and door frames; and for mold-ings, cabinets, and glued-laminated beams. Resin from its bark goes into glues and photographic supplies, and shredded bark makes a garden mulch.

The wood of Douglas fir is so desirable that the species has been widely introduced in other parts of the world. Jack Woods tells me it is grown in Chile, parts of Argentina, New Zealand, Germany, Switzerland, Turkey, Spain, and France, where it is becoming the primary introduced species. Here, in its home, most of the old-growth forests have been logged, and we will soon be dependent on timber grown in replanted and managed forests. Scientists in British Columbia, seeking to determine how second-growth Douglas fir wood compares with the old-growth timber, formed a task force that reported its conclusions in 1989. The participants, from Forintek Canada (a national research and development agency), the Research Branch of the B.C. Ministry of Forests, and the Pulp and Paper Research Institute of Canada, examined the wood of trees from six stands on Vancouver Island and concluded that "second-growth coastal Douglas fir harvested in 50 to 70 years will have physical, mechanical, and chemical properties substantially different from the old-growth resource harvested today."

The difference between old-growth and rapidly grown Douglas fir is in the proportion of mature wood to juvenile wood. The younger wood, which is not as dense and so not as strong, forms a core around the pith from the base to the top of the tree. Observing a young tree, you will see that it has branches almost to the ground. These living branches contribute to the formation of wood that has wide annual rings with a higher proportion of earlywood cells, mak-ing it a less dense wood. An older tree begins to lose its branches. Where the living crown ends, mature – denser – wood is formed. Silviculturists are now asking if pruning the lower living branches will speed up the transition and produce a larger proportion of the kind of wood that we have come to expect from Douglas fir. Jack Woods notes that, in the past half-dozen years since the task force report was written, attitudes have changed. He says pragmatically, "The juvenile wood problem is not that big. A lot is being cut now and used. If you provide just juvenile wood, I can guarantee people will find ways to use it."

THE FIRST HOUSE my husband and I bought in Vancouver had kitchen counters and a built-in dining table made of wood – a rich, warm wood in wide, thick planks with a grain like puddles of amber liquid. When I saw that table, I imagined a happy family eating

Fog envelops the lower levels of a Douglas fir forest near Mount Baker in Washington State.

there, and that is what we did for nearly a quarter of a century. In a renovation we replaced the kitchen countertops, but I kept the wood and have had some of it made into a useful table that sits beside me now as I write. I had been told the wood was fir, a name that struck me as vague, and so when I read about Curtis Erpelding, who has been in business as a furniture-maker since 1977, I decided to visit him at his home outside Port Orchard, Washington, and see the fine furniture he makes from Douglas fir. "You can tell Douglas fir by the orange color," he said, and I recognized my countertops. Some woodworkers find the wood garish and want to cover it, but Erpelding enhances it with a diluted varnish sealer and coats of Danish oil: "I like that carrot-orange color."

Erpelding creates effects by manipulating the grain. Douglas fir lays down a harder latewood and a softer earlywood, recognizable in the dark and light lines of the annual rings. If the wood is flatsawn – imagine a log run round end first through a bread-slicer – the top surface of the board will show an irregular, sinuous pattern. If the wood is vertical-cut or quartersawn – imagine a log cut along its length into quarters and the quarters cut as a pie would be – the grain that shows on the top of the board will be the annual rings, which form regular, parallel lines. "I love the grain of it – the waviness of the flatsawn grain – and the linear, graphic effect in vertical grain. You can play with the grain in ways you can't with other woods." Erpelding has played around, too, with limbs that have fallen from his Douglas firs. He has tried to turn them on a lathe, but the difference in the density of the spring and summer woods makes turning difficult.

Like woodworkers everywhere, Erpelding is concerned about the forest that supplies his raw materials. He was among a group of 200 Northwest environmentalists that arranged to have a 730-year-old Douglas fir log from the Olympic National Forest go on tour across the United States to publicize its concern for the coast's vanishing old forests. He started using construction-grade Douglas fir partly because he didn't have a lot of money and partly for ecological reasons. "There's not a lot of this wood left and people were wasting it on outdoor things or interior woodwork that would be painted. Using it for fine furniture was a statement that this wood should be respected more than it is."

THE TWO GREAT pioneering botanical collectors on the Pacific coast of North America met once in London in 1824 when the younger was preparing to visit the same lands that the elder had seen three decades before. David Douglas was the 25-year-old Scottish botanical collector hired by the Horticultural Society of London to gather plant specimens in northwest America. Archibald Menzies was a 70-year-old retired physician who had traveled with Captain George Vancouver from 1792 to 1794 as surgeon and botanist.

Menzies was the first person to climb 13,680-foot Mauna Loa on the island of Hawaii, and even though his botanical forays along the North American coast were often curtailed by Vancouver's need to get on with his survey, he was the first trained botanist to see and describe the giant trees of Pacific North America. He seldom ranged far from the coast and, as a result, never did see the giant sequoia.

Having entered Juan de Fuca Strait after sailing north from Monterey, the Vancouver expedition was exploring around Admiralty Inlet and Puget Sound in Washington State in 1792. On May 2 Menzies wrote in his journal that he had seen the Sycamore Maple (bigleaf maple), the American Aldar (red alder), and the Oriental Strawberry Tree (madrone or arbutus). On May 9 he reported an oak (Oregon white or Garry oak): "As intervals of fair or clear weather permitted, parties strolld along the Beach & met with some Oak Trees on which account our present situation was called Oak Cove." In June he saw Native women wearing garments woven from the prepared bark of the "American Arber Vitae Tree" – western red cedar – and he described "a very indifferent shelter" fashioned from mats of cedar bark thrown over a frame of rough sticks. On June 24 the *Discovery* sailed out of Howe Sound "past a number of Islands some of them pretty large & all covered with Pines." The islands were Anvil, Gambier, and Bowen (where I live), and the pines – the word was used by Menzies as we use conifer or evergreen – were western red cedars and Douglas firs.

In 1795 he took stems of Douglas fir back to England and gave some to Aylmer Bourke Lambert, who was vice president of the Linnaean Society, a body that included the world's greatest scientists and of which Menzies was a member and, later, the president. An expert on pines, Lambert published *A Description of the Genus Pinus* in 1803, in which he included two of Menzies's discoveries: he classified coast redwoods as *Taxodium sempervirens* (an evergreen that resembles a yew) and Douglas fir as *Pinus taxifolia* (a pine with leaves like the yew).

David Douglas was a child of four when Lambert's work was published. After some formal education, he was trained as a gardener, apprenticing at the Earl of Mansfield's gardens near his birthplace, Scone, Scotland, and by age 23 taking charge of the Botanical Garden at Glasgow. He was hired by the Horticultural Society of London as a collector and made his first expedition – four months in New York State and Upper Canada – in 1823. In July 1824, having boned up on botany, zoology, and geology, and having visited Menzies and others for advice, he sailed again as an employee of the Horticultural Society on a Hudson's Bay Company ship bound for the Columbia River. On April 7, 1825, the *William and Ann* safely crossed the treacherous sandbar at the mouth of the river. From the ship's deck Douglas saw a hemlock, a balsam fir, and "a species that may prove to be *P. taxifolia*," the tree that had been described to him by Menzies.

With the help of the Hudson's Bay Company's Dr. John McLoughlin, Douglas established himself at Fort Vancouver, about 100 miles from the mouth of the Columbia, and spent two years exploring and collecting. In the Cascade Mountains he admired the noble and silver firs – "the grandest trees of the tribe." On a mountain west of present-day Roseburg, Oregon, he found a tree he had long sought. Unable to climb its tall, limbless bole, he was shooting at the cones when eight Natives appeared. Noticing that one was stringing his bow and another sharpening a flint knife, Douglas cocked his guns and offered tobacco in exchange for more cones. The Natives left and Douglas fled with three cones and a few twigs of the world's tallest pine tree, the sugar pine, which he named *Pinus lambertiana*, after the author of *Genus Pinus*.

In 1826 he shipped plants to his employers and, the following year, sent his living collection to England by ship and carried seeds there himself, traveling overland across North America. After two years in England, he was rehired in 1829 by the Horticultural Society to explore the interior of California and by the Colonial Office to make magnetic and geographical observations. Douglas returned to the West Coast where he collected plants in Oregon, California, British Columbia, and on the islands of Hawaii, until his accidental death there in 1834 – he fell into a bullock pit and was gored and trampled.

Douglas had always made certain that samples of his specimens were sent to his friend and patron Sir William Hooker, who in 1833 published *Flora Borealis Americana,* using the West Coast collections of Archibald Menzies and David Douglas. Douglas introduced more than 200 plants previously unknown in England. Between them,

Douglas and Menzies have given their names to 124 plant species and varieties, but none has been more significant on this coast than the tree named for both of them – *Pseudotsuga menziesii,* commonly known now as Douglas fir.

It is fitting that a Douglas fir has been growing since 1827 on the grounds of Scone Palace, where David Douglas was an apprentice gardener, and that a grove of Douglas firs marks the spot where he perished on a Hawaiian island.

The Douglas fir at Scone Palace in Scotland, grown from seed gathered on the Pacific coast by David Douglas on his first expedition between 1825 and 1827.

THE EARL OF MANSFIELD

Lords of the Land Garry Oak/Oregon White Oak

IN BRITISH COLUMBIA where Douglas firs, western red cedars, and western hemlocks are as familiar as hydro poles, there is a giant of a tree that many people may never see. Mainland British Columbians, visiting the province's Gulf Islands and southeastern Vancouver Island, or crossing the border into Washington, Oregon, or California, are sure to notice what is for them an arboreal aberration – a gnarly tree whose lichened and mossy limbs bend and contort at odd angles but produce a broad, rounded canopy of glossy green leaves. From time to time they might see clusters of people in the vicinity of these trees, engaged in activities that suggest a devotion no less than that of the Celtic Druids who worshipped similar benedictory branches.

The tree the Celts revered was an oak, which they called *quer cuez*, meaning "fine tree." From *quer cuez* came the Latin word for oak – *quercus* – and our scientific designation for a genus that has anywhere from 300 to 500 species. The Pacific Northwest *Quercus*, which grows from California to British Columbia, was described by the naturalist David Douglas in 1825. A few years later he recorded the same tree growing in California and saw aboriginal peoples eating the tree's acorns after seasoning them for a year in water-filled pits dug near streams and lakes. The tree that produced this disagreeable smelling and far from palatable food he named *Quercus garryana* for Nicholas Garry of the Hudson's Bay Company.

Keeping the historical connection, Canadians call the tree Garry oak. It is their only native *Quercus* west of the heartland province of Manitoba – the largest, longest living broad-leaved deciduous tree in western Canada and one of the rarest trees in the country. Growing only in the dry coastal Douglas fir zone, which occupies 0.3 percent of the land of British Columbia, it qualifies as a Pacific giant because of its longevity and size: it can live for 400 to 500 years and can exceed 120 feet in height. On the mainland there are only two small groves in the Fraser River Valley – one on a shale outcrop at Sumas Mountain, near Abbotsford, and the other on a rock promontory outside Hope. Garry oaks grow beautifully on the islands in the Strait of Georgia – for example, Saturna, Saltspring, and Hornby

An amazingly tall Quercus garryana *(Garry oak, as it is commonly called in Canada) towers 115 feet above a road intersection in North Saanich on Vancouver Island.*

with its Thousand Oaks Grove, a large contiguous stand on a former ranch (being subdivided by a developer who says he is trying to protect the trees). On the east coast of Vancouver Island – from just north of Courtenay, south to Victoria – the tree was, and to an extent still is, a local emblem.

The Canadian presence, which as we shall see is unique, is a tailing-off of the longest north-south range of any western oak. Crossing into the United States, *Quercus garryana* becomes Oregon white oak, a name that indicates its former abundance on the hills of western Oregon and distinguishes it from red or black oaks, the acorns of which take two years to mature compared to one year for white oaks. The largest specimens once rose in the northwestern part of the state in the Willamette Valley and along the Columbia River. At Portland stumps six feet in diameter suggest what the pioneers must have seen.

Oregon white oak now grows around Puget Sound and in a swath parallel to the I-5 freeway all the way to San Francisco, taking an eastward detour along the Columbia River between Washington and Oregon, drawing closer to the Pacific coast near the California border, and climbing into the North Coast and Klamath ranges in northern California. Farther south and inland in California it becomes shrubby. It is Washington State's only native oak and Oregon's principal species, but the only native oak in that state with round-lobed leaves. Of the nine tree oaks in California, this is the one that ventures a considerable distance north.

Travelers on the interstate easily recognize the pleasing rounded crowns of *Quercus garryana* near the highway or at a distance in a farmer's field. At any time of year the tree is outstanding. In spring its male, pollen-bearing flowers develop in hanging, yellowish catkins while bright red female flowers, the future acorns, grow in the axils of the emerging leaves, which will have five or seven rounded lobes, a pebbly upper surface, and a hairy underside. If the tree inhabits a meadow or savanna, it may preside priestlike over a congregation of blue camas lilies and yellow buttercups. In summer healthy leaves are dark green – shiny on the upper surface, lighter and matte underneath. (Too often, unfortunately, the leaves are scorched or spotted.) Because the tree is intolerant of shade, the leaves seek the light at the outer reaches of the branches, a growth habit that creates the familiar broad, ball-like canopy. If a tree is among Douglas firs, it will reach up for the light, producing a narrower, round crown. Deep in autumn, when photosynthesis has ceased, rust-colored leaves stand out against the green of conifers, and the tree's complement of lichens and mosses will be revealed.

OPPOSITE
A Garry oak – the largest, longest-living broad-leaved deciduous tree in western Canada – reigns over a meadow of blue camas lilies in Victoria, British Columbia.

FOLLOWING PAGES
In previous centuries Oregon white oak (the common name of Quercus garryana *in the United States) reached enormous size along the Columbia River near present-day Vancouver, Washington. This tree is a substantial remnant.*

When the foliage has followed the acorns to the ground, the eye can trace unhindered an architectural form that is both patterned and idiosyncratic. While the main thrust is upright, huge limbs angle down or are bent as though the tree had been pulled simultaneously by competing forces. In old age Oregon white oaks are equally remarkable. As the authors of *Trees to Know in Oregon* say: "They draw our attention, for they're lords of the land – offering us endless visual pleasure."

Motorists need detour only a short distance away from the insane interstate in Oregon or Washington to enter an asylum of oaks. Ten minutes took me, for instance, to Ridgefield, Washington, and a wildlife refuge with 400- to 500-year-old *Quercus garryana*. Close to the Columbia River and its cool breezes, the refuge is an important stopover on the Pacific Flyway: hundreds of thousands of waterfowl spend the winter or pass through on their way south. Even the parking lot (at the end of North Main Avenue) possesses a fine oak with a circumference of 15 feet, 10 inches, but across a railway bridge and along the 1.9-mile nature trail are scores of other substantial specimens. I stood in a sun-dappled cloister of five 100-foot-high trees on the rim of a hill. Overhead, blue sky outlined individual leaves in the canopy, as if each one had commandeered a place in the sun. Many of the trees have enormous limbs that begin high on their trunks and curve to the ground where they flatten out or begin to grow back upward, inviting a loiterer to sit and bounce gently – very gently because, in dry summers, oak trees will suddenly shed large limbs, a habit noted by Native peoples who would not make camp beneath them. By mid-August fuzzy soft brown buds have appeared at the point where the leaves meet the stems and at the leading tips of stems. Acorns, some green, some brown, hang from short stalks, in pairs or singly. Longer than wide, they are about the size and shape of the first joint of an average woman's thumb. Some trees bear reddish-brown speckled galls that contain a developing wasp larva. Children like to stomp on these pop balls or oak apples.

The Ridgefield site is a moist woodland – just one of the settings in which *Q. garryana* succeeds. Elsewhere it grows in open forest stands of conifers and other broad-leaved trees. On rocky outcrops it assumes a shrubby form. This oak can survive in an area that receives as little as seven inches of rain a year. In fact, it withstands drought better than any other tree on the North Pacific coast, a characteristic in its favor if our climate were to become warmer and drier. Conversely it will tolerate having its roots in standing water on riverside plains that are flooded from time to time. Oregon white

Native peoples used fire to keep the savannas open and free of conifers so that they could cultivate the camas lily, the bulb of which was a staple food.

oak is not as well suited to the more pronounced Mediterranean climate of California. Just as a straw will collapse if a thick liquid is sucked through it, so the leaves of an Oregon white oak, which aren't as thick and waxy as those of other California oaks, are unable to tolerate the pressure created when in a dry atmosphere water is drawn up forcefully from the soil and through their tissues. As a result, the tree grows best in the northern part of the state, near rivers, or at higher elevations.

The British Columbia oak landscape is often parklike, and in these meadows, which are quite different from those along the American West Coast, biologists have found 1,000 species of plants and animals, among them more than a fifth of the rarest plants in the province. Ninety species of vascular plants rare in British Columbia grow only in Garry oak meadows, notably at the southeastern end of Vancouver Island, which has been an oak habitat for thousands of years. By the time Europeans arrived at the present site of Victoria, British Columia, a former Great Age of Garry oak was waning, but the trees were still a distinguishing feature of an extraordinary landscape. James Douglas, who chose the site of Victoria for a Hudson's Bay Company fort in 1842, wrote to a friend that it was "a perfect Eden in the midst of the dreary wilderness of the Northwest coast. . . ." He established Beacon Hill Park as a public preserve. Today this city-owned 190-acre park is a favorite place to admire Garry oaks, some of them 350 years old. In the open meadows at the Fort Victoria site, Native peoples had hunted deer and harvested the camas lily bulb, which was a staple food. In fact, they called the area Camosun, meaning "a place to gather camas." As did the aboriginal peoples in the United States, they maintained the savannas by setting fires to clear away underbrush and discourage conifers that would eventually overtop the oaks.

Even today the Garry oak landscape, where it remains natural, is wildly strewn with pink shooting stars, purple satin flowers, blue violets, and brown chocolate lilies, among dozens of flowers that unfold from February to May. But just as the first settlers took advantage of the open landscape for their forts and fields, so today the builders of highways and houses find the open Garry oak landscape enticing. The attention of local communities was aroused in 1988 when a grove of oaks on Christmas Hill in Saanich, near Victoria, was felled for a condominium development. One result was the Garry Oak Meadow Preservation Society, a group of 100 people devoted to preserving the trees and their remarkable ecosystems. The society promotes the passing of tree-protection bylaws, holds work parties to rescue native plants and to eradicate the noxious

White fawn lilies decorate a meadow around St. Mary's Church in Metchosin on Vancouver Island. The southeastern end of the island has been a Garry oak habitat for thousands of years, and some of British Columbia's rarest plants are associated with the tree.

non-native Scotch broom, and collects acorns to grow seedlings to replace the oak trees that have been lost.

Eric Redekop is a director of the society. A 36-year-old part-time teacher of history and geography, he has embraced the cause of old oak habitats – not just the tree, but the entire package. He refers to Garry oak as "the charismatic macroflora of the ecosystem" and thinks it is a mistake to be seduced by the sexiness of the tree: "We can't just focus on the tree. We do that at the peril of the whole system." He may spend time contemplating the subtle impact of a Garry oak on its environment – for instance, how a heavy, low-slung branch moving in the wind rubs against a rock and, over time, shifts moss to a moister, more beneficial place. "The yin-yang of tree and rock," he says. And he is moved by the vulnerability of trees whose continuing existence is so much a function of human whim: "When I see one of these giants, I think, Well, old man, what have you seen? What winds have blown through your branches? They have this permanence, but like us, they are fragile." His own garden, on a smallish corner lot in Victoria, testifies to his concern for preserving the less showy bits: he has made it into a plant refuge, containing 43 native species recovered from road-widening projects. The bulk of the plant material rescued by Redekop and other society members, who diligently sifted soil to find it, has been held in district greenhouses until it can be replanted beside finished roadways.

Scotch broom was introduced to the island 150 years ago by a Scot who successfully sprouted three seeds. Despite its admittedly cheerful yellow flowers, the shrub is now a naturalized scourge, the bane of oak tree stewards all the way to California because it crowds out the desirable native species that characterize the tree's ecosystem. Others try to deal with broom by burning it, but the Garry Oak Meadow Preservation Society favors backbreaking techniques that have to be undertaken in the cold-weather months. From October to January they hold broom bashes in which volunteers pull stems, trying not to disturb the soil too much, or they cut them below the first lateral root, which effectively discourages resprouting. In late 1995 Victoria had its first citywide broom bash, called Operation Clean Sweep. Volunteers brought loppers and saws to eight broom-ridden locations and hauled away mountains of the nasty weed.

Yet another problem with British Columbia's Garry oak population is what dendrologists call recruitment – the survival of juvenile trees. As Eric Redekop puts it, "We're not seeing any little guys." From the production of acorns through to the survival of saplings, regeneration is unpredictable. In some years Victoria's oaks produce few acorns – as happened in 1993 for no known reason. In

Four-hundred-year-old Oregon white oak can be found in quiet groves near the Columbia River. Quercus garryana is British Columbia's and Washington State's only native oak and the principal oak species in Oregon.

other years every acorn will be infested with filbert worms (a moth) or filbert weevils. If a tree has lost its leaves in summer because of an insect infestation, there will be no energy from photosynthesis to ripen its acorns. But in a good year thousands of ripe acorns will fall. It is important that they fall before the leaves. Because acorns have no mode of transportation – other than rolling downhill or being carried away by birds, animals, or tidy gardeners – they must survive where they land, and sitting under, rather than on, leaf litter keeps them moist and protects them from freezing.

Robert Hagel, who supervises the Canadian Forest Service's greenhouse operations at the Pacific Forestry Centre in Victoria, says that in nature Garry oak acorns readily germinate soon after dropping in September. The shell cracks and an embryonic root, a radicle, emerges. Within weeks this radicle extends deep into the soil. Then the rooted acorn sits under leaf cover until the following spring when its cotyledons, or embryonic leaves, appear. In its infant years it will compete for moisture with nearby vegetation. "If it is severely droughted," says Hagel, "it will not make it."

Unlike California's blue oak, which is not regenerating at all, many Garry oak acorns do germinate and begin to grow. Pam Kranitz, a research scientist with the federal government's Environment Canada, says you don't see them until you look for them. At one site on Department of National Defence property, she found a huge old tree surrounded by "a wall of 10-centimeter-high seedlings." Not all will survive, but she says we have to ask ourselves if we want oak woodland or oak savanna. "You only need one tree per hectare for an oak savanna."

Victoria may find itself with a regiment of oak recruits. In the past few years as many as 10,000 seedlings have been produced through Project Acorn – a cooperative effort of the Canadian Forest Service and the Garry Oak Meadow Preservation Society. The society's members gather the acorns. Rob Hagel sows those that have sprouted and sorts the remainder by dropping them into water. Dried-out or weevil-ridden acorns will float; viable ones will sink. Hagel soaks the sinkers for 24 hours – to ensure adequate moisture content – and places them in cold storage until, with the help of volunteers, they can be planted in tall, narrow containers that accommodate their long taproots. Hagel was surprised by the growth rate of Garry oak in the greenhouse: in nature a one-year-old seedling might grow two inches, but indoors there are usually two or more annual growth flushes. Year-old seedlings can be anywhere from six inches to three feet high, with most reaching eight to 10 inches. The seedlings have been distributed for planting by individuals and various

Oak acorns crack and send out an embryonic root in the fall. The acorns spend the winter covered by their parent tree's leaves, which protect them from freezing until spring when they can recommence growth.

municipalities. As well, to restore vegetation after highway construction, the provincial Ministry of Transportation and Highways planted several hundred year-old seedlings, encasing them in plastic tubing – their own personal greenhouses. After only two years, many have reached six and a half feet. As they produce their characteristic fan of secondary roots, they will become wind-firm.

With all its natural enemies, it is fortunate that *Quercus garryana* is not considered commercially important. Its wood has been cut for shipbuilding, flooring, furniture, and firewood. Because its heartwood does not readily rot in soil, it was used for fence posts, which might last for a century, and as a result, the tree was nicknamed "post oak." It is a hard wood, so hard that Pam Kranitz, who was attempting an age-distribution study on Vancouver Island, says she broke three increment bores on 15 trees.

In the final analysis we should acknowledge that the Celts got it right. This *is* a fine tree, a tree that pleases the eye, nourishes the soul, and creates a haven for other plants and animals. Words like *beneficent, nourishing, nostalgic* come to mind, but Dr. Kranitz found the best description for *Quercus garryana* when she stepped outside the realm of science. "It's one of my favorite trees," she said. "When you sit under it, there's a comforting feeling. It feels maternal."

SIRENS AND THE THOUGHT OF WILDFIRE draw me from my bed on summer nights when we haven't had rain for weeks and ignorant trespassers have allowed illegal bonfires to spread to dry mosses on our oceanside cliffs. I am the more nervous for having read about the fire in northern Idaho in August 1910, which author Donald Peattie described as the worst forest fire in history. It grew out of 3,000 small, unattended fires – something less likely to happen now – but still I think of fire-generated winds that knocked forest rangers off their horses, of superheated air that volatilized resins in the western white pines and created clouds of inflammable gases, and of burning boles uprooted by sucking winds and tossed around like torches.

This spring I shall clear away the woody debris to create a less flammable zone around our house. I hope I am learning something of value from the use of fire in the giant sequoia groves in California, where controlled fires are set to decrease the hazards of big fires and to stimulate the regeneration of the giant trees. After years of fire-prevention programs and Smoky the Bear advertising, scientists were able to demonstrate that devastating crown fires were more likely in the absence of regular small fires.

Fire is, in fact, a friend of some trees. Without it Oregon white or Garry oak cannot keep Douglas fir from encroaching upon its woodlands and savannas. In a conifer forest mature Douglas fir, with its thick bark, is the beneficiary of fire. Because older seedlings need full sunlight, and because its seeds germinate best on mineral soil, Douglas fir needs fire to clear out western hemlock in the understory and to burn off duff on the forest floor.

Fire has been a frequent visitor to the giant sequoia groves, a history researched by scientists in the Laboratory of Tree-Ring Research at the University of Arizona. Examining trees in five groves, one researcher took 500 cross sections from 90 dead trees, sanding them so that all the rings could be exactly dated. He found one scar indicating a fire in 1125 B.C., but most of the fire dates began about 500 A.D. The average number of burns per tree was 63.8, as many as 46 fires occurred in one century, and fire-free intervals were always less than 13 years. The official suppression of fire by government agencies could be seen in the drop in scars beginning in 1860. Because of frequent, naturally occurring blazes, the groves had long held steady with trees and shrubs in various stages of succession. When fires were suppressed, California white fir began to dominate the shade-intolerant sequoias in the understory.

It has been said that the most serious impact human beings had on the giant sequoia groves was the elimination of fire. With their thick, nonresinous bark and high crowns, large trees may be damaged but will survive many burns, and their chief aim in life – the regeneration of their species – will be improved. As a result, late spring and fall blazes are now set by the park service; they are not so hot as to damage the trees but hot enough to burn off the understory, which resets the successional pattern in the sequoia's favor.

Fire does the sequoias another favor. Like some other conifers, the tree has serotinous cones – cones that remain closed, keeping their seeds until conditions are right for their dispersal. Fire dries out these cones, and the seeds are released to fall upon a newly cleared mineral-soil seedbed.

If fire can be a friend in this way, so can an insect. In 1968 scientists discovered a beetle that also plays a role in causing the seed cones of giant sequoia to open. *Phymatodes nitidus* is a long-horned, wood-boring beetle that lays its eggs on the outside of the cones. The larvae hatch and eat their way into the cones. As they move around inside, they may cut the connections that bring water to the scales. One by one the scales turn brown, dry out, and shrink, allowing the seeds to fall.

THE FORESTS ARE FULL of less friendly insects – defoliating, wood-boring, cone-infesting pests that attack the giant-tree species. One that has had an expensive impact on forest management in British Columbia is *Pissodes strobi* – the white pine weevil – which destroys the vital leading shoot of its host. As a result of widespread infestation throughout the province, the planting of Sitka spruce has been cut back since the 1970s. Current research at the Canadian Forest Service's Pacific Forestry Centre began with weevil-resistant trees in an effort to understand why some insects avoid them and why those that feed on them are unable to make eggs. A long-range plan, developed by entomologist Dr. Tara Sahota and his team, is to feed insects a diet incorporating extracts from the whole bark of resistant trees to see if some substance from the tree has an effect on their ability to produce eggs.

More than 800 insect species associate with *Quercus garryana*. Only 140 are herbivores, but of those, 48 feed only on this oak. The tiny, nonstinging jumping gall wasp (*Neuroterus saltatorius*) is native to the western United States but was not known to occur in British Columbia until 1986. Less troublesome at home, jumping gall wasps have had a widespread impact in the province, and for a time, it was impossible to find an oak that had not been affected. Female wasps insert eggs into the lower surfaces of leaves. The developing larvae induce the formation of mustard-seed-sized galls on the lower leaf surface, turning heavily infested leaves brown in the summer. When the larva inside the gall is fully grown, the gall falls to the ground, where it "jumps" as a result of the movement of the larva. Dr. Robert W. Duncan, with the Forest Insect and Disease Survey of the Canadian Forest Service, has found that the jumping gall wasp is attacked by several insect predators and eight species of parasitoids (the larva of a parasitoid develops within the body of another insect, killing the host). He has also noticed that the galls on the leaves of some trees fail to grow beyond an early stage. "We suspect that elevated phenol levels in the leaves of some trees prevents further development of the gall," he says.

The oak-leaf phylloxeran – an import from Europe – attacks and may eventually kill Garry oaks susceptible to it. Like an aphid, the insect pierces and sucks sap from the underside of leaves. Heavily infected leaves turn brown and drop, completely defoliating and weakening the tree. Ten native insect predators prey on the oak-leaf phylloxeran. Because not one appears to control it, scientists are considering the release of a European predator. It is a move with precedent: a parasitic moth and a parasitic fly imported from Europe and released in 1979 to 1981 are controlling the winter moth, which throughout the seventies defoliated most of the region's Garry oaks.

THE TREE LOOKS LIKE a monster from a movie about triceratops and troglodytes. It hulks in a grove a short distance off Highway 101 where a narrow stretch of Olympic National Park hugs the Pacific coast, six miles north of Kalaloch in Washington State. This western red cedar could be an imaginary construction designed to frighten children lost in the forest at night. It isn't so much a tree as an accumulation of boles, burls, buttresses, and roots jammed together to form a mass 64 feet, two inches in circumference. Without ducking my head, I walk under what appears to be a root coming from the trunk and arching over to the ground like the flying buttresses of Notre Dame in Paris. Above the root is a western hemlock, which has a two-foot-wide trunk and is attached like a Siamese twin to the host tree's bole. In the morning sun the east side of the red cedar looks like a cafeteria for shrubs and salal, and I wonder if this is a living tree or merely a standing dead support for other vegetation. But in the crown, green-leaved branchlets catch a bit of sunlight, and with my binoculars I see that they are indeed the fernlike sprays of western red cedar.

The Kalaloch tree is one of the largest red cedars on the coast, and like many old members of its tribe, it has long since ceased to be a thing of beauty and has become a curiosity. Old western red cedars often lose their symmetrical, narrowly conical crowns. Stressed by drought, the top of the tree will die and be replaced by a new top emerging from below. Because this may happen several times over many years, aged western red cedars are compared to candelabras, although a bunch of celery stalks might be a closer description. The American co-champions certainly have that appearance. The Nolan Creek cedar was discovered in 1978 during logging of timber on state land south of Forks, Washington. The tree was spared because of its great size, and it has spent nearly two decades presiding first over the stumps of its former companions and now over the young trees that have replaced them. In 1994 Robert Van Pelt, the coordinator of Washington's Big Tree Program, reported that the tree was nearly dead, its only live root having been

Western red cedar was called the tree of life by Europeans, but to the Native peoples of the coast it was "Rich-Woman Maker" or "Long-Life Maker."

FOLLOWING PAGES
Totem poles at Ninstints, British Columbia, on tiny Anthony Island (Skun'gwaii) in the Queen Charlottes, were carved from the finest western red cedar boles.

cut during the installation of a walkway to protect the tree. It is still listed, however, in the 1996-97 National Register of Big Trees with its co-champion, the Quinault Lake cedar.

THE NATIVE PEOPLES of the West Coast sought out only the best-formed red cedar boles for their totem poles and canoes. On the island where I live off British Columbia's Lower Mainland, Isaac Tait took me into the circle of western red cedar and Douglas fir in his side yard where he was carving his latest work from an 850-year-old slab of western red cedar. Tait is a Nisga'a from the Nass River in northern British Columbia, and this carving is of a classical Native symbol – a Wealthy Moon Mask. The finished piece will be a 42-inch circle with a human face surrounded by a wide decorative border, the entire surface inlaid with copper and abalone. Although, as he says, "There is nothing new here," he has brought all his artistic sensibilities to the task of drawing out of the wood what he envisions. Despite his carefully calculated proportions, he had just encountered an unforeseeable problem buried in the aromatic heartwood. Right on the tip of the nose of the central face, a brown spot appeared and, as he carved, it got bigger. It is strange to think of that knot, the remains of a branch that started and stopped growing five or more centuries ago, to think of it hidden deep in the log and showing up on this crucial point. Tait was taking it calmly, even though his client – BASF Canada – had to have the mask in about six weeks for the opening of a new corporate building in Raleigh, North Carolina, and here it was sitting under a tarp on the other side of the continent waiting for the rain to stop so Tait could recommence carving.

This red cedar wood came from a six-foot-wide, 12-foot-long section of old-growth tree donated to his client by MacMillan Bloedel, the B.C. forest company. Tait was pleased to be working on old-growth wood. It is stronger than second-growth, he says, which with its wider annual rings produces a rippling effect in the carving and doesn't hold his highly sculptural detail. When he works with red cedar, Tait prefers green wood, which has been recently cut and has not dried out. The difference between carving it and dry wood is comparable to working with room-temperature or refrigerated butter, he told me. On this piece Tait was working outdoors because he had to hose it down regularly. "If I left it in the sun, it could dry and split in half an hour, but if I wet it and keep it covered, it will retain the moisture." Red cedar holds a lot of water; Tait has seen chainsawn logs bleed a bucket of red liquid.

Carving professionally for 12 years since he was 18, Tait learned

OPPOSITE
Whippy and woebegone, the branches of western red cedar are unlike the robust upper arms of a Douglas fir. The tree's tiny cones gather in clusters and resemble pert rosebuds.

FOLLOWING PAGES
Two cohabiting giants of British Columbia's Khutzeymateen Inlet – the grizzly bear and the western red cedar.

the intricacies of working with red cedar from his father, Norman Tait, a carver of international reputation whose totem poles stand in front of the Field Museum in Chicago and the Native Education Centre at the University of British Columbia, the latter a project on which Isaac was an apprentice. In working with big slabs of red cedar, the carver is always trying to prevent checking or cracking, which happens when thicker wood creates more tension. He must maintain a uniform thickness throughout the block, carving it down, as he says, "all over at the same time." His problem with the discolored nose had to be resolved in the same careful way, by sinking the entire face three inches deeper into the wood until the flaw disappeared. When the features of the mask were finished – when they had acquired what he calls "a focused look" – he began to thin out the back, again in order to lessen tension and prevent cracks.

Tait practices an art that goes back centuries, using the same techniques that coastal peoples devised to render great red cedar logs into totem poles. In their monumental forests the First Nations of the West Coast found and left uncut the Douglas firs and western hemlocks that newcomers from Europe would fell with such enthusiasm. Haida carver Bill Reid, writing in *Out of the Silence*, explains that stone axes and wooden wedges could not bring down the tough, hard Douglas firs, and the people eschewed the hemlocks and Sitka spruce, the woods of which were "splintery and hard to work and weathered badly." Instead they turned to the lackadaisical giant with the softer heart, a tree that – to quote photographer Bob Herger – makes you think, "Oh, you poor thing."

Woebegone in aspect, with bark that resembles long tresses of hair, and draped in whippy, slender withes that hang down like vines, western red cedar nevertheless grew tall and straight from a fluted base, sometimes with lower trunks wide enough to make two canoes, with a third one coming from the tapered top. The tree didn't have to be felled to be of use. Bark could be stripped and made into instant boards, boxes, and cooking pots. Softened by pounding, bark was the raw material for nets, ropes, mats, clothing, baskets, and even baby diapers. The withes made heavy-duty baskets, stout rope, and a good fiber for sewing the corners of bentwood boxes. The roots were woven into baskets and used for sewing and tying. Even planks could be wedged out of standing trees. And with their relatively soft wood, the giants could be cut down by a team of men, sometimes slaves, chiseling beaver-style around the trunk or weakening the base with a controlled fire.

Who knows what the ancient peoples of the West Coast would have been without western red cedar, but with it – and the abundant

The stringy bark of western red cedar is easy to recognize. Native peoples stripped it off in long lengths, pounded it soft, and used it for clothing or even for diapers.

food of the ocean – they were wealthy. Some Northwest Coast peoples called the sheltering tree "shabalup," which means "dry underneath." Others addressed the tree as "Rich-Woman Maker" or "Long-Life Maker," honorifics echoed by Europeans, who called it the Arbor-Vitae, "the tree of life." English speakers call it a cedar, a term they apply loosely to many conifers that are not really cedars. For instance, eastern red cedar is a member of the juniper genus, and yellow cedar is a false cypress, a *chamaecyparis*. Western red cedar is a member of yet another genus – *Thuja*. This name, an ancient Greek word from a verb meaning "to bear scent," was first applied in 1576 to an American conifer introduced into Europe. In 1737 Carolus Linnaeus saw two similar trees in a collector's garden in Holland. The one from Asia he named *Thuja orientalis* (it is commonly known as oriental cedar) and the one from North America became *Thuja occidentalis* (our eastern white cedar).

A half century later, when Archibald Menzies collected samples of an "American Arbor Vitae" on the west coast, the scientific binomial *Thuja plicata* was given to western red cedar. *Plicata* refers to its flattened, folded, scalelike leaves, which look pleated or interwoven. Together many leaf-covered shoots form a fernlike frond, which droops gracefully but presents a flattened plane to the sunlight. The seed cones are one of the species' most recognizable features. They sit in clusters several inches back of the tip of a shoot complex, pointing up and bent back slightly, as though they were trying to escape to the center of the tree. Green when ripe, they are about the size and shape of a pistachio nut and resemble an unfolding rosebud.

Thuja plicata ranges along the Pacific coast from Humboldt County in California to southeastern Alaska. An interior range of shorter length is physically separate from the coastal trees. The largest specimens are found on the Olympic Peninsula of Washington State and on Vancouver Island in British Columbia. A species that prefers rain to cold, western red cedar doesn't grow to the same large size above elevations of 5,000 feet, nor is it frost-resistant, sometimes being damaged but not killed by freezing spring or autumn weather. While alluvial flats and old creek beds are its favorite sites, it will grow in moss bogs and in drier climates on rich soil.

Western red cedar is not often found in large unmixed stands. It likes to keep company with any of the coastal trees and is more tolerant of shade than most of them, except western hemlock. It lives longer – 1,000 years being not uncommon, and 2,000 a possibility. The largest western red cedar in the United States or Canada, the

The leaves of Thuja plicata *look pleated or interwoven. They present a splayed frond to the sunlight but droop somewhat sadly in cold or snow.*

Cheewhat Lake tree on the west coast of Vancouver Island, is approaching the end of its second millennium. Unlike most other conifers, it produces new foliage along the trunk – epicormic branches – and retains its lower limbs even when they are shaded.

Conifers are generally the most genetically diverse of living things, but for many years now scientists have pointed out what seemed to be a lack of genetic variation in western red cedar. Typically researchers examine seeds, looking at proteins called isozymes. As late as 1981 they were finding no or little variance in isozyme patterns of seeds from western red cedars from different West Coast provenances. But more recently people like John Russell, a geneticist in the Research Branch of the B.C. Ministry of Forests, have taken a different approach. "It's hard to believe that a tree that is spread so wide in its range has no variation," he told me. "So we started looking at the tree itself. We started growing trees and looking at the pedigree of the kids, who their mom and dad were and the area they came from." They *are* finding genetic variation between populations, for instance between trees from north and south Vancouver Island, and between kids with different parents within a population. But this variation is less than that in other conifers.

Except for widely separated populations – trees in California versus those in the northern B.C. interior – there is little evidence that western red cedars have evolved genetic stategies related to climate. Dr. Russell explains that this has to do with the natural history of the species, which was a latecomer in the succession of forest trees after the last Ice Age, possibly being present in locations such as the north part of Vancouver Island for only 2,000 years. In a mild, wet climate there was less selection pressure, and the trees lived for a long time, with fewer generations to produce a fine-tuning of adaptive genetic variation.

Western red cedar has a characteristic that allows seed from one population to grow at a different latitude. Other conifers tell by day length (the photoperiod) when it is time to set their buds – that is, when they should stop their growth. Silviculturists know that because of this sensitivity to the amount of daylight, the progeny of Sitka spruce from Alaska will not thrive in California and vice versa. But western red cedar does not produce buds and is not as regulated by photoperiods. It is more in tune with the temperature and will resume growth on sunny days in November.

Yet another peculiarity of western red cedar is that it has purged itself of mechanisms that prevent self-pollination (see "Conifer Sex," page 109). It will "self" successfully and produce normal seedlings.

But, at about age five, inbred trees grown in field trials start to fall behind cross-pollinated trees. John Russell suggests that selfing allowed western red cedar to proliferate despite its solitary habit and to survive when small stands were fragmented in passing Ice Ages.

The technical data compiled by modern science about the wood of *Thuja plicata* confirms what the aboriginal Northwest Coast peoples learned by observation and experience. Scientists have found that the thujaplicins and tropolone derivatives that abound in old-growth western red cedar are toxic to decay-producing fungi. Or as Isaac Tait told me, "The wood had natural oils so you didn't have to preserve it by oiling." With a specific gravity lower than that of Sitka spruce, Douglas fir, western hemlock, or yellow cedar, western red cedar was the tree of choice for canoes that carried entire families and several tons of cargo. That the wood was flexible helped canoe-makers shape the sides by steaming – forcing them apart and holding them open with thwarts, which served as seats for the paddlers.

The ease with which red cedar can be split is a property put to use today by the manufacturers of roofing shakes and shingles. For pre-Iron Age peoples it meant lumber – smooth, broad planks for the walls and roofs of longhouses, furnished inside with platforms, partitions, screens, storage shelves, and bentwood storage and cooking boxes. To take planks from felled logs, they began by inserting wedges into a split at the butt end of a log. Gradually, by hammering in more wedges along the side of the log, workers could push the split down its entire length, making planks of great width and length. Again, the wood's flexibility could be exploited in bending planks of suitable thickness into boxes.

With such a past it is disturbing to think that the species' future is in question. Participants at a conference in Vancouver in 1987 met to explore the question, "Western Red Cedar – Does It Have A Future?" The issues were economic in their focus: How can you reduce the costs of logging on the steep slopes where the tree grows and reduce breakage when trees are felled on these slopes? Will breeding programs result in better growth and survival? What is to be done about the reduced levels of natural preservatives in second-growth wood? How can mills get more clear-grade lumber from each log? How can pulp processors overcome the corrosive effect the wood has on their digesters? And should we just stick to growing Douglas fir because it is strong, and western hemlock, Sitka spruce, and Pacific silver fir because they have nice white wood and make excellent pulp?

There is no doubt that the wood of western red cedar is still sought for its aesthetic qualities – its silvery weathered look on the exterior of West Coast houses and its aromatic warmth when applied to interior walls. With luck and prudence there will be second-growth wood for our descendants' homes. But how narrow our vision is of the tree that once built a culture. Carver Bill Reid, in *Out of the Silence*, captures the reverence of his people for a tree that gave long life and made women wealthy: "Oh, the cedar tree! If mankind in his infancy had prayed for the perfect substance for all material and aesthetic needs, an indulgent god could have provided nothing better."

In February tiny black heads on the tips of western red cedar branches
signal a resumption of reproductive activity.

The Sexually Shy False Cypress

Sargent Randally — named for Randall Dayton and Ally Gibson, the MacMillan Bloedel engineers who found it — is the world record Alaska or yellow cedar. Growing in the Memekay Valley of British Columbia, northwest of Campbell River on Vancouver Island, this astonishing tree sets new standards for the species. The current American champion, located on the Olympic Peninsula, is 124 feet high with a circumference of 37 feet, six inches. Sargent Randally is 203 feet tall with a circumference of 36 feet, three inches. Despite a dead top, it is still in good condition — likely to go on for another 300 or 400 years, according to Gibson. The tree has been protected by MacMillan Bloedel, ribboned off in a nice stand of old-growth cedar.

Canadians know this dramatically drooping conifer as yellow cedar; in the United States it is usually called Alaska cedar. Both common names are misleading but were probably given because the tree has fragrant wood like the true cedars. Native only around the Mediterranean and in the Himalayas, true cedars have evergreen needles borne in dense clusters on woody pegs. Their large, oblong seed cones sit upright on the branches. Alaska or yellow cedar, with its scalelike leaves and small, round cones, is clearly not a cedar. It belongs instead to the cypress family where it is grouped in the genus *Chamaecyparis*, which (to compound the confusion) is known as the false cypress genus. The species' name — *Chamaecyparis nootkatensis* — records the location of its first sighting, Nootka Sound, the favorite safe harbor of Captain Vancouver on the west coast of Vancouver Island. This is the only false cypress native to Canada, but it has an American relative known as Port Orford cedar or Lawson cypress.

Yellow cedar, the name I know it by, is John Russell's favorite tree. A geneticist at the B.C. Ministry of Forests research station at Cowichan Lake on Vancouver Island, Russell says, "I like the look of the tree. It's beautiful-looking at a younger age." He also likes this tree's out-of-the-way habitats, which take time to find but lead him into beautiful areas of the country. Yellow cedar is often a loner, taking advantage of openings among other trees or growing where no other tree will, hanging on a steep, rocky slope or settling in at the edge of a bog. Most of its range is within 100 miles of the coast, but in Oregon, Washington, and on the British Columbia mainland, climbing up to 2,000 feet will just bring you into its territory. It can be found at elevations of 5,000-plus feet in Washington and British Columbia. On the west coast of Vancouver Island and from Knight Inlet, British Columbia, north into southeast

Alaska and Prince William Sound, the tree descends to sea level.

Words such as *drooping, sorrowful,* and *shaggy* have been used to describe it. The lower bows do sweep down, sometimes touching the ground, but its droopy look comes primarily from its foliage-bearing twigs, which depend in a limp-wristed fashion. It is, however, a graceful tree that is often chosen as an ornamental species for gardens. Growing extremely slowly, the species lives for a long time, with specimens reaching 3,500 years of age. British Columbia's big-tree hunter, the late Randy Stoltmann, listed verified ages for seven yellow cedars in the province ranging from 1,693 years to 1,294.

It is not difficult to tell western red cedar from yellow cedar. The cones are perhaps the quickest means of identification. Western red cedar's seed cones are shaped like rosebuds, while those of yellow cedar are ovoid with four or six scales, each with a peculiar triangular spur in the center. Although both trees have scalelike leaves, those of western red cedar are flattened and tightly pressed together. Some people say you can see a butterfly outlined in white on the back of the leaves. Yellow cedar's are folded rather than flattened. They can flare out and be a little prickly, and no pattern appears on their undersides. (It is useful, however, to know that the backs of Port Orford cedar leaves are marked with a little white *x*.) The bark is another giveaway: yellow cedar's is scaly on young trees and gray and stringy on veterans. Western red cedar has a smooth, shiny juvenile bark and a reddish, stringy mature bark. Like western red cedar, yellow cedar doesn't set a bud – it doesn't stop its growth before winter. It is more plastic in its behavior, taking advantage of warm weather to grow a little.

When it comes to sexual reproduction, yellow cedar could be said to have cause to look sorrowful. It has a longer reproductive cycle than other conifers – taking 28 months from the time cones begin to be produced until the seed is released. Each cone has only a few seeds and they don't germinate well. As John Russell puts it, "The tree tries but doesn't like to have sex in the wild." As a result, most trees planted in artificial reforestation are from rooted cuttings rather than from seedlings. What yellow cedar will do effectively is regenerate by layering. Its branches bend down and root where they touch moist soil. Russell tells of stands of yellow cedars felled in avalanches and later massively regenerating from layered branches.

Yellow cedar's wood is harder and heavier than that of western red cedar. It has a fine texture, a uniformly straight grain, and takes a beautiful finish. It has long been a favorite of boat builders, partly because it endures damp conditions but also because it is light and strong. The wood is also used by architects who don't care whether it is false cedar or false cypress – merely how lovely it looks.

83
—
FALSE CYPRESS

*Called yellow cedar in Canada,
and Alaska cedar in the United
States, this graceful conifer has a
hard time reproducing sexually
in the forest.*

IN THE YARD AT K Ply Inc. in Port Angeles, Washington, black cottonwood logs sit in house-high stacks, awaiting a transformation. They are barnacle-encrusted and smell of the sea on which they have been rafted from western Washington or from Kitimat in British Columbia. Looking at their butt ends, I find it hard to imagine a higher use than what awaits them. Each log is stained and splotchy, its light-colored sapwood surrounding dark, discolored heartwood. Not a tree to inspire a cabinetmaker. Their size, however, is impressive. Cut near Smithers, British Columbia, some of these 50- or 60-year-old second-growth trees are four feet in diameter; two-thirds are what Chuck Lockhart, K Ply's resource manager, considers "good-sized." He estimates some trees have three growth rings to an inch, which means that every three years these trees have added two inches to their width, a rate of growth that beats all other trees on the coast.

Black cottonwood is a worthy and, until recently, underutilized and underappreciated giant of our West Coast forests. The largest broad-leaved tree in western North America, it can grow at a truly phenomenal rate, equalling in 50 years the height and girth that a Douglas fir will attain in a century. Because it reproduces readily and can be induced to hybridize, it is an ideal subject for genetic experiments. Forest geneticists have already produced a cottonwood hybrid that doubles the normal volume put on by black cottonwoods. Also, given the suitability of the wood for pulping, plywood, and lumber applications where strength is not a factor, it is no wonder that forest managers are turning to black cottonwood hybrids as an easily managed addition to conifers.

Some of the trees in K Ply's yard were cut 18 months ago and have floated for a year in a B.C. river where they demonstrated the remarkable capacity of black cottonwood to regenerate from its own vegetative parts. Almost any part of the tree will regenerate: roots produce suckers, stumps produce sprouts, fallen trees become nurse logs. "I saw some wood recently – floating logs with trees three feet tall growing on them," Lockhart says. He has seen trees

The largest broad-leaved trees in western North America, black cottonwoods grow from Alaska through to northern California, reaching great heights at phenomenal rates.

sprout from woody debris pushed underground by skidders or from branches shoved into the ground by hand. Foresters know that if they cut down a young tree, its stump will produce sprouts for several years, providing a cheap supply of new trees. Silviculturists point out the unusual ability of growing trees to abscise – to cut off – small, green-leaved shoots, which may root where they fall or be carried downriver to start a new stand.

Lockhart knows black cottonwood as only a practical person can. "I've just finished processing a million board feet, I've remanned [remanufactured] it myself, and I've worked as a bureau scaler." A burly man, with a full head of graying curly hair, he wears his jeans short and fringed at the bottom – "if a jagger catches in the hem, it can drag you" – and his shirt sleeves rolled up above the elbow, revealing arms the size of respectable tree limbs. Looking at the black cottonwood he had bought in British Columbia, he thinks about the tree. "A guy told me they have a pulse. When you start to cut the tree, water pumps out. I haven't seen it pump out, but the sapwood holds a lot of water. You go home wet at the end of the day." One of the problems with cottonwood is something called tension wood, which produces an unattractive woolly surface when it is sawn. "It's timber-bound," says Lockhart, explaining that this happens when a tree growing on a slope tries to straighten itself. Wind in the forest is another factor affecting the wood: "Where it's windy, trees will grow with a twist. Instead of growing up, they have to pull themselves straight. We have seen trees in the forest doing a slow twist. We have watched it – where every tree seems to twist the same way."

The bark of black cottonwood intrigues Lockhart; it seems tough, he says, and you can peel it like the bark of western red cedar. He picks up a piece three inches thick and peels off a strip, revealing a pinkish underside. "People tell me they carve on it," he says. In cold regions, he has noticed, trees produce a thicker hard bark; other people have said it is hard enough to spark when sawn.

Aesthetically black cottonwood seems to have invested all its effort in its two-toned leaves, which more closely approach a pleasing valentine shape than those of other poplars. Donald Peattie, the eloquent author of *A Natural History of Western Trees*, considered black cottonwood to be the most beautiful western poplar: "And when the great drafts blow up and down the Columbia gorge . . . the black cottonwood comes into its full beauty, for on one side the leaf blades are darkly glittering, on the other almost silvery white with rusty veins. If you look down on this scene from the hills and highways, the trees seem, like the sea, to break into whitecaps before the

86

—

GIANTS

On one January day in 1994, 3,769 bald eagles were counted sitting on the thick branches of black cottonwoods in the Squamish River valley north of Vancouver, British Columbia.

wind." Most people find the species impressive in autumn when the leaves are golden.

Black cottonwood is vigorously sexually reproductive. Male trees bear pollen catkins and female trees seed catkins, which ripen into hanging clusters of small green globes. Usually in May the globes split open and release many tiny seeds attached to long, cottonlike hairs, which loft the seed into the air or keep it afloat on water. The seed-laden fluff drifts into piles or even into your nose, leaving no doubt that the tree is aptly named. The seed is highly viable and, landing in a moist spot, will readily germinate. Given moisture and light – black cottonwood is extremely intolerant of shade – a high percentage of seedlings will appear. One problem with naturally regenerating plantations of poplars is that too many seedlings survive: as many as 30,000 stems have been counted on a single half acre. "It's real prolific," as Lockhart says.

Black cottonwood is sometimes known as western balsam poplar. It is closely related to eastern balsam poplar, and their ranges overlap in the interior of Yukon, British Columbia, and Washington State. Taxonomically black cottonwood is hard to pin down. Some authorities regard it as a separate species, naming it *Populus trichocarpa*. Others consider it to be a subspecies of *Populus balsamifera*, and they designate this cottonwood *Populus balsmifera ssp trichocarpa*. *Trichocarpa* comes from the Greek *thrix* (a hair) and *karpos* (fruit) and refers to the species' hairy seed catkins (I have also read the word might have something to do with the fact that the fruit splits into three parts when ripe).

The species grows from Alaska through to northern California, mostly west of the Rockies, although in Canada its range extends into Alberta and in the United States into Idaho and Montana. Giant individuals usually inhabit the bottom lands of major rivers. In Alaska the largest trees grow along the Chilkat River near Klukwan in the southeast. In 1965 a 101-foot black cottonwood was found west of Klukwan on the Klehini River. Chuck Lockhart worked for several years as quality control and sales manager for Klukwan Forest Products, a successful Native village corporation that logs on Long Island southwest of Ketchikan and owns K Ply in Port Angeles. He says Alaska's black cottonwoods look nice, but they are often hollowed by decay that begins when the water-laden trees freeze and crack.

By far the greatest volume of black cottonwood in British Columbia is around inland Prince George and in the Nass and Skeena river valleys northeast of Prince Rupert. According to B.C. Ministry of Forests research scientist Michael Carlson, the largest specimens in

Because they are vigorous in their sexual reproduction and can regenerate from most vegetative parts, black cottonwoods form into crowds, like this autumnal group near Clearwater, British Columbia.

Black cottonwoods grow to great size on the floodplains of the Columbia River in Washington and the Fraser, Homathko, and Kingcome rivers in British Columbia.

FOLLOWING PAGES
The champion black cottonwood is on Skumalasph Island in the Fraser River near Chilliwack, British Columbia. In this area American reseachers found superior female trees for their hybridization trials.

the province grow near Stewart, across the border from Hyder, Alaska. Touring the area recently by helicopter, he spotted and photographed a tree on the Bell-Irving River he estimates to be 300 years old, seven feet through at the base, and approximately 150 feet tall. In British Columbia, south in the species' range, superior specimens grow along the Fraser River near Chilliwack. It was from this location that Washington researchers, looking for "healthy trees with straight stems, above average height and volume growth, and fine limbs," selected two female trees as parents in recent hybridization trials.

By report black cottonwoods 225 feet tall once grew in the Olympic Peninsula, and many 200-footers were found in Oregon along the Columbia River. The current American national champion is in Oregon's Willamette Mission State Park. Measured in 1994, it is 158 feet tall, with a circumference of 26 feet, eight inches, and rates 506 points. This means that the mother of all black cottonwoods grows on Skumalasph Island near Mission, British Columbia. Measured in 1992, the 142-foot-tall B.C. champ has a circumference of 30 feet and rates 527 points.

At places along the northwest coast – Alaska's 49,500-acre Chilkat Bald Eagle Reserve and Washington's Skagit River Bald Eagle National Area – black cottonwoods provide daytime roosts for huge numbers of bald eagles as they feed in the winter months on the bodies of spawned-out salmon. But on one January day in 1994 the world's largest counted convocation of bald eagles – 3,769 – gathered in the Squamish River valley north of Vancouver, British Columbia. The phenomenon is said to depend upon the big trees that grow along the river. After gorging on rotting fish, the birds perch during the day in the largest black cottonwoods, whose thick branches support their weight, and at night they return to their conifer nests. On a January day in 1996 I watched our neighborhood bald eagles pushing north up Howe Sound against a blustery wind. The Squamish River was, as the eagle flies, less than an hour away, and I hoped they were going to sit in the black cottonwoods for the 10th annual count, which I later heard yielded only 1,859 eagles.

Like other western broad leaved trees, black cottonwood has not had great commercial value on a coast blessed with abundant coniferous species. But in recent years, with the depletion of easily obtainable conifers, interest in cottonwood has increased. Its strengths – rapid juvenile growth, early sexual maturity, and an energetic yearly reproductive effort – are counterbalanced by a susceptibility to decay, breakage, frost cracks, and a leaf rust that diminishes its productivity. As far back as 1910, a researcher in Ireland

used black cottonwood in an attempt to crossbreed poplars to create a more vigorous strain. In 1978 researchers at the University of Washington and Washington State University joined in a cooperative program to study the variations in natural black cottonwood populations and to enhance desirable characteristics by selective breeding and hybridization with other poplars. The goal is an improved tree that can be farmed in short rotations.

A principal investigator in that study is Thomas Hinckley, a tree physiologist at the University of Washington's College of Forest Resources. He says that a great deal is known about the genetics of black cottonwood. "We actually have a linkage marker map, which in some ways is related to the gene structure of the chromosomes. From this map we can understand the inheritance of morphological, physiological, and growth traits and disease resistance." The ease with which black cottonwood can be cloned makes it one of the forest geneticist's preferred tools: "You can copy it faithfully thousands of times," says Dr. Hinckley. Summing up with an allusion to *Drosophila*, the genus used extensively in genetic research, he adds, "It's the fruit fly of trees."

Researchers around the world are interested in discovering how *P. trichocarpa* can improve their native poplars or are considering planting hybrids created on the West Coast. Michael Carlson, of the forest biology section of the research branch of B.C.'s Ministry of Forests, has escorted a Swedish scientist on a tour of black cottonwood provenances. The Swedes, he says, want to plant poplars in the southern part of their country, which is at about the same latitude as northern British Columbia. The available crosses of *P. trichocarpa* and *P. deltoides* do well on the coast and around protected lakes, but the Swedes need trees that have the cold tolerance of more northerly black cottonwoods. Since Dr. Carlson is trying to make a cross that will succeed in the province's colder areas, he may be able to provide what the Swedes need. In the winter of 1994-95 forestry workers, hanging out of helicopters, collected twigs from 650 black cottonwoods and balsam poplars in 17 river drainages. After a period in storage, the cuttings were rooted and grown. They are now in the ministry's clonal archives in Vernon and serve as a source for the development of hybrids.

Cees van Oosten, a poplar expert with the B.C. timber company MacMillan Bloedel, says that international interest assures the future of native black cottonwoods. "We will always need the black cottonwood as a resource to go back to for breeding material," he explains. Van Oosten admits that back in the sixties few people at MacMillan Bloedel cared about black cottonwood, but in the mid-eighties the company initiated a small trial of the tree on bottom lands along Vancouver Island's Salmon River and asked its research division to explore uses for the wood. It was pointed out that pulp for paper needed less chemical brightening when black cottonwood was added to the usual western hemlock/balsam fir mix. In producing a glossy paper for advertising inserts and magazines, the company will add poplar into the pulp mix when its plantation-grown hybrids are ready in 2003 or 2004. Van Oosten says the hybrid improves the opacity of paper and has short fibers that fill in holes in the sheet.

MacMillan Bloedel has 1,000 acres planted on Vancouver Island, in the Fraser Valley, and Washington State and will harvest trees aged between 10 and 12 years so that the operation falls under agricultural rather than forestry regulations. "It's like growing corn, but the rows are farther apart," says van Oosten.

Until MacMillan Bloedel's recent venture, the only company growing and using cottonwood in the province had been Scott Paper Ltd., which in the late 1950s planted a hybrid poplar from Europe – a genetic mix of a North American and a European poplar – alongside native black cottonwoods. In the 1960s the company had 2,500 acres of these rather slow-growing and nicely formed hybrids, which were good for veneer. In 1985 the company obtained British Columbia's first hardwood Tree Farm Licence, comprising 25,000 acres, half of it usable land on the floodplains of the Fraser, Homathko, and Kingcome rivers. Here they planted faster-growing *P. trichocarpa* and *P. deltoides* hybrids from the Washington research program. Now, with additional plantings on farm licenses, the company is creating its own supply of poplar hybrids and naturally regenerating black cottonwoods, which it adds to a kraft pulp to make household paper products.

Other uses that have been proposed for black cottonwood and its hybrids range from generating electrical energy to purifying waste water by irrigating trees with urban sewage effluent. Generally companies have confined their ventures to the more prosaic, such as the production of plywood. K Ply Inc. in Washington produces paper-covered plywood with three, five, seven, and eleven plys for signs, concrete forms, exterior siding, and interior walls of modular buildings (some of it pressed, ironically, with a wood-grain design).

The transformation of a log into sheets of wood is almost too fast to see. One moment I was looking at a debarked log slightly longer than the width of a sheet of plywood. Then clamps grasped it at both ends so it could revolve against a blade, which smoothed it to a uniform diameter and then peeled it, in a process that resembles the unrolling of toilet paper. In no time all that remained was the core, which looks like a fence post and will be sold as exactly that.

Moving a little down the production line, I saw the veneer being carried away from another rapidly shrinking log. Sometimes it takes as much as 20 seconds for a long, unbroken sheet to slip past, revealing the hidden, discolored heart of a tree that once delighted with its shimmery leaves and sweet-smelling springtime buds. With that image fading rapidly, I watched the veneer slide into a machine called a clipper where a scanning lightbar detected seriously flawed sections to be cut out by a blade that descended like a guillotine. The veneer sheets were heat-dried and the knotholes filled with thin oval plugs before being built by hand into a wood sandwich, with alternate layers running lengthwise and crosswise. The plywood sheets are covered top and bottom with smooth paper and heat-pressed to finish the process.

Lockhart, a man who cares that trees are well used, is practical about the fate of black cottonwood here at K Ply. "We're making plywood," he says. "We're taking what some people have called a weed and we are making a good product out of it."

AMONG THE TREES of North America's West Coast, the Pacific yew is a giant only in its recent celebrity. For a tree that hides away in the shadows of our forests, it has had its day in the sun. With any luck it will survive the exposure.

Taxus brevifolia is an exceptional tree. It is classed with the conifers but doesn't have cones; instead, each dark green seed is encased in a fleshy, bright red aril, which looks like a pimento-stuffed olive with the colors reversed. It is also classed as a softwood but has hard wood, which is highly valued by the makers of canoe paddles, archery bows, and musical instruments. While its foliage and seeds are poisonous, its bark and foliage have for centuries provided medicinal preparations for human use.

We have long been careless of this unobtrusive tree. Where we have found it, usually growing alone in stands of western hemlock, Douglas fir, and other Pacific coast trees, we have trashed it or sold it cheaply for fence posts, ignoring the many higher uses for which the wood is suited. Ironically by 1989 Asian buyers had pushed the price of yew wood to $6,000 U.S. a thousand board feet (the same quantity of Douglas fir fetched $500), but by then the race was on to locate Pacific yews in the northwestern United States and to strip their bark to make the cancer-fighting agent now known as paclitaxel.

The Pacific yew is often inconspicuous in the shaded regions of the understory and is something of a hermit. If you stand beside one yew tree, I was told, you will probably not be able to see another one. Because of this solitary habit and the fact that the species has male and female trees, there is some doubt about how the pollen and seed find each other. Al Mitchell at the Canadian Forest Service's Pacific Forestry Centre in Victoria, British Columbia, says pollination may be accomplished by wind or perhaps by birds, but it is difficult to understand how two trees a quarter of a mile apart could make contact. Underlining the fact that little is known about the Pacific yew, he has found no published work on the reproductive ecology of the species.

Pacific yews also reproduce by sprouting or by layering – branches or even tree tops pressed to the ground for a time will root and grow, although the resulting trees may be quite twisted. The Pacific Northwest Research Station in Oregon reported a 12-inch-wide stump surmounted by sprouts and surrounded by seven trees, which were the result of layering.

Pacific yew's short needles (that is why it is named *brevifolia*) are the darkest green of our evergreen trees. The tips of the needles are pointed, which is unusual, but they aren't sharp like spruce needles. Light exposure affects the shape and color of the needles. Flat, wide, deep green ones grow in the shade; thick, narrow, bronze ones are found in the sun. This adaptation to changing light environments explains in part why the tree can live as long as 800 years and reach heights of 60 or more feet in forest gaps.

The Pacific yew is one of eight closely related species of the genus *Taxus*. The Latin word comes from the Greek *taxon*, meaning a bow, although two Dutch authors suggest that the name may be related to the Greek *toxon*, an arrow that had been steeped in yew sap. The Celts, Greeks, and Romans knew that the European yew was poisonous and that its wood made strong spears and flexible bows. On the Pacific coast the First Nations peoples fashioned yew wood into a variety of similar weapons and tools (including razors to remove underarm hair); ate the berries as a contraceptive; and employed the bark or foliage to treat bronchitis, stomachaches, and skin cancer.

Unfortunately for our yew, the wisdom of folk medicine led the National Cancer Institute (NCI) to include the tree in its screening of 35,000 plants for cancer-fighting compounds. Although a North Carolina chemist had isolated a complex compound called taxol from the bark and noted its tumor-suppressing activity in 1966, his work was ignored by the NCI until a team of New York pharmacologists unraveled taxol's mode of action in 1979. Taxol was synthesized to the active ingredient – paclitaxel. Human trials began and, within a decade, it had been shown that paclitaxel extended the lives of women with ovarian cancer (which kills 12,000 American women annually). Later it was found promising in the treatment of breast, skin, and lung cancers. In 1991 the NCI awarded Bristol-Myers Squibb an exclusive contract to develop paclitaxel, and the USDA Forest Service and the Bureau of Land Management (BLM) gave the company the exclusive rights to Pacific yew harvested on federal lands.

Environmentalists were alarmed. Taxol is a chemical the yew produces as a defense against insects and disease. It is found in every part of the tree, but because the U.S. Food and Drug Administration had approved only the bark as a source, wholesale stripping of trees began. Unsustainable quantities of bark were needed: two grams of taxol, enough for one treatment, required the bark of 10 trees with 10-inch-diameter trunks. In 1991 alone, 790,000 pounds were collected, killing about 40,000 yews on U.S. Forest Service and BLM property. In 1992, 1.6 million pounds were harvested and the two government agencies predicted that in the next two years, 10 percent of all the

Pacific yew would be taken. Subsequently, through a complex and novel semisynthetic process, a precursor to paclitaxel was extracted from the renewable needles and twigs of the English yew. Synthesized to paclitaxel, it was formulated into the drug taxol. In December 1994 Bristol-Myers Squibb announced it was no longer dependent on Pacific yew bark. It has since been reported that many of the trees harvested for their bark were cut on timber-sale lands, where they would have been destroyed, anyway. Now care is being taken to replace harvested trees, and U.S. federal agencies have developed plans to retain genetic diversity in the species and to ensure its survival.

It was a close call for *Taxus brevifolia*. Just as the bows and arrows of medieval armies drained forests of European yew, so the poisoned arrow we found to shoot against cancer threatened the earth's last significant population of native yews. As we have often done, we destroyed a tree that had no immediate or perceived monetary value, and when we discovered that it was the source of something useful, we exploited it to the point of near-ecological disaster.

Western yew, the solitary hermit of our coastal forests, now has a good chance of surviving the recent rush to extract medicinal ingredients from its bark.

HALF A CENTURY AFTER David Douglas toiled up a mountain south of the cascades on the Columbia River and found two new fir trees – one of which he called *nobilis* and the other *amabilis* – botanists were saying the latter, the *lovable* or *lovely* fir, didn't exist. Visiting European botanists had failed to find it. In 1879 Georg Engelmann, the American physician, botanist, and plant collector, writing his *Botany of California*, pronounced *Abies amabilis* a myth. A year later Engelmann and two colleagues – Charles Sargent, a director of the Arnold Arboretum at Harvard University, and Charles Parry, a botanist – went exploring south of the present-day town of Hope on the Fraser River in British Columbia. On what is now called Isolillock Peak, at an elevation of 4,000 to 5,000 feet, they saw, as the *Journal of the Royal Horticultural Society* reported, "a beautiful, unfamiliar Fir, which they at once recognized as the long-lost 'Amabilis' – the same that Douglas had first made known fifty-five years previously."

A conservation officer at B.C. Parks headquarters in Victoria told me he doubted that story because *Abies amabilis* – Pacific silver fir – is not that hard to find. But it does seem to be true that this species prefers more inaccessible locations, as photographer Bob Herger discovered. Reluctant to climb Isolillock Peak in search of the myth-breaking firs, Herger went instead to the south end of Chilliwack Lake and explored Ecological Reserve No. 98, which touches the British Columbia-Washington border. At an elevation of 2,000 feet and straddling the Chilliwack River where it drains out of the lake and into the United States, this is one of the province's most beautiful and little known old-growth forests, with many large western red cedars. It was on the riverbank in this reserve that a record grand fir – 234 feet tall and 20 feet, 10 inches in circumference – was found in 1985. Toward the end of a long day in this forest, Herger found what had been described to him as an awesome grove of silver fir on the Canadian side of the border. He was, if not disappointed, puzzled. "Where the cedars were growing," he said, "there was a feeling of ease, of everything being in sync. There in the *amabilis* grove it was chaotic and very dark, not as friendly. The trees

Once declared to be a myth, amabilis, or Pacific silver fir, proves it does exist. This stand is in British Columbia's Ecological Reserve No. 98, south of Chilliwack Lake.

seemed to be just trying to survive. They were very mature trees and they looked like white telephone poles with a rounded top of foliage."

Had Herger flown over these trees, he might have seen crowns that look like puffy mushrooms. At least that is the way they appear to Jim Pojar, a forest ecologist at the B.C. Forest Service's research station at Smithers, who greatly admires what he calls an underappreciated species. "On the north coast [of British Columbia] and at higher elevations, it's a nice tree aesthetically," he says. Although there is a great deal of *amabilis* growing in the province, he points out that on the south coast you have to get to higher elevations to see it. He agrees that silver fir forests are dark: "It's hard to get anything darker than a young hemlock forest, but old-growth *amabilis* tends to be darker than other types of old-growth forest." The shade-casting, parasol-like crowns of silver fir contribute to the forest's darkness but in no way inhibit regeneration. The species is one of the most shade-tolerant in the Pacific Northwest. It will form a climax forest at mid-elevations of its range, or it will be codominant with western hemlock, which also thrives in shade. Its crown shape and thick, rigid, upright branches have adapted it to heavy snow loads, which either slide off or cause less breakage than on a tree such as Douglas fir, which holds its branches closer to horizontal.

Of the nine species of *Abies* – the true firs – native to North America, two are distributed generously on the coast. (A tip for British Columbians: there are no true firs in the Queen Charlotte Islands.) Pacific silver fir is best developed at middle and upper mountain elevations, but farther north on the B.C. mainland, into southeastern Alaska, and on the west coast of Vancouver Island, it comes down to sea level. It can still be found in the Cascade Mountains of Washington and Oregon, where Douglas saw it, and in the Olympic Mountains of Washington. At lower elevations the ranges of silver fir and grand fir overlap, but the latter is primarily a lowland species whose largest specimens are in the Olympic Peninsula rainforest. The grands range narrowly up the coast from Sonoma County in California, widening into the Cascades in Washington and Oregon, and narrowing again to the west coast of the B.C. mainland and to the east coast of Vancouver Island, stopping at about 50 degrees north latitude. An inland range, where the trees are not as tall, extends from southern British Columbia to northeastern Oregon.

Two other firs, which grow to a large size, are uncommon near the coast, although subalpine fir (*Abies lasiocarpa*) does occur in the Olympic Mountains and on Vancouver Island. Noble fir (*Abies procera*), the other tree that Douglas saw, is a Rocky Mountain and Cascadian

With parasol-like crowns, Pacific silver firs form dark forests where their straight-sided trunks and whitish-gray bark stand out like telephone poles.

species, which produces the tallest fir trees in the world and the best fir wood.

Distinguishing one fir – or balsam, as they are sometimes called – from another can be difficult. Cones, which so quickly identify other species, are almost impossible to examine on firs because they perch upright on branches in the top quarter of the crown and break up scale by scale rather than falling whole to the ground. Jim Pojar warns about silver fir cones, which at 3.5 to 5.5 inches long are the largest of the fir cones. Purplish in maturity, fat, barrel-shaped, and loaded with pitch, they are clipped off by squirrels and will come down, according to Pojar, "like a grenade." He's never taken a hit, but "it's been very close." The slightly smaller grand fir cones have scales that look squished compared to the broader silver fir scales. Both types pose a problem in seed-cone collection programs: because they break up and disperse their seeds, they must be gathered when they are still somewhat premature.

Needles are key to identifying *Abies* species. A park ranger told me to look for the distinctive "little bum shape" – a notch in the rounded ends of the grooved needles. A problem is that tall, old firs may have no foliage close to the ground. By experience Bob Herger has learned to lie on his back and examine the canopy through a pair of binoculars. Often he searches the ground for twigs brought down by cone-hunting squirrels. That might lead to error, however, because true firs produce a sharp-tipped foliage in the crown, which curves up as though protecting the cones. Grand fir has long needles arranged in two distinct horizontal rows on the twig, like a double comb. Silver fir has four rows – two ranks of longer needles spread out flat and perpendicular to the side of the twig and two rows of shorter needles on the top of the twig, leaning noticeably forward. While grand and silver fir needles have a white bloom only on their lower surfaces, noble and subalpine fir needles have bloom on both surfaces. Noble fir needles are bent where they meet the twig and are said to resemble hockey sticks (as do those of Douglas fir); subalpine fir needles are less than an inch long and surround the twig. The needles of all firs leave a unique circular scar on the twig when they are broken off – a good clue to identifying the genus.

All firs, because of their lovely foliage and resinous odor, are prized for Christmas trees. The resin, found in blisters on the bark of young stems, is used in preparing microscope slides. Oils from the foliage are used in medicines, and the bark resin is said to soothe insect bites and prevent infection in small cuts.

Commercially less important than other conifers, the firs produce a light-colored wood that goes mainly for paper pulp and is also

Grand fir needles are grooved on top, have a rounded, "little bum"-shaped tip, and a white bloom on the underside. They are long and sit in two distinct rows on the stem.

sold as lumber with western hemlock. Jim Pojar says the timber of silver fir has been disdained, perhaps because old trees are not sound, but if the trees are grown in 100-year rotations, they will produce good structural lumber. Fir wood finds a market in Japan because it is white.

Grand firs that grow in the open have pleasing symmetrical crowns with branches coming to the ground. As they rise to champion heights in the 230-foot range, the trees' crowns thin out but still have branches well down their trunks. The species can sprout new – epicormic – branches where old ones have been lost. Because it is susceptible to rot, it lives for only 250 to 300 years. Seldom found in pure stands, grand fir plays a couple of successional roles in a mixed forest based on its lesser shade tolerance. In some habitats it can be the dominant climax species; in others it will be a long-lived member of a series of ecological communities. On the coast grand fir grows rapidly in youth, as quickly as Douglas fir. It can reach 140 feet in only 50 years. In England where grand fir has been cultivated, 40-year-old plantation trees frequently grow as fast as, or faster than, Sitka spruce and Douglas fir.

Silver fir, on the other hand, needs 10 to 15 years to hit its growth stride. The trunks, with their whitish-gray bark and straight sides, rise to heights of 200 feet (the American champion is 217 feet tall), and individuals do live to be 500. Sometimes in a wind the branches of silver fir rotate 180 degrees, and the silvery undersides of the needles make these trees look, as Donald Peattie wrote many years ago, "like shining angels." Indifferent to frost, even as a seedling, it grows at upper elevations, as in the Cedar River watershed southeast of Seattle. Here Findley Lake sits in a horseshoe-shaped, glacial basin at an elevation of 3,700 feet. Pacific silver fir and mountain hemlock grow at lake level, while warmer slopes to the west, south, and east are clothed in western hemlock, western red cedar, and noble fir. In this montane forest a number of researchers are trying to understand how tree species deal with high-elevation environments. One observation – a surprise – is that root growth begins in mid-February when the soil is still cold and covered in snow.

Thomas Hinckley, the tree physiologist at the University of Washington's College of Forest Resources in Seattle, is doing research in four stands of variously aged Pacific silver fir. Without ascending very high, he can study a species that has some of the characteristics of lower-elevation trees yet experiences colder temperatures and a significant winter snowpack. In this forest some of the silver firs are 500 years old but have been growing at a moderate rate for only 230. The tree can remain suppressed in a stand, waiting until a gap

Pacific silver fir has several ranks of needles. The two rows of shorter needles on the top of the twig lean noticeably forward.

opens in the canopy to recommence growth. Dr. Hinckley describes small 20- to 50-year-old individuals that are the size of three-year-old Douglas firs. His research forest has three levels of trees, with the tallest being 100 to 150 feet.

In the canopy individual branches have been isolated in tent chambers so that researchers can study respiration, which is one way a tree has of redressing the cost of photosynthesis and of providing the energy to move its sugar compounds to where they are needed. This basic research is aimed at determining what controls respiration: where it happens in the canopy; how much there is in the tree; whether it stays the same as trees or branches become older; and whether it is affected by the seasons. Dr. Hinckley's studies in the Cedar River watershed are based on work for the Environmental Protection Agency (EPA), which is trying to assess the damage ozone may do to western coniferous forests. Ozone, a common pollutant in the Northwest, leads to a suppression of photosynthetic activity. As the tree attempts to repair its carbohydrate deficit, respiration increases. The EPA has data on the effect of ozone on seedlings, but not a lot is known about the sensitivity of older trees to airborne environmental stresses.

I asked Tom Hinckley what he notices about the upper canopy of the silver fir. "You get to see patterns of symmetry that you would never have believed existed," he said. "You can take a cone or a shoot of a tree and mark out the paths that the needles or the scales take, and there is a symmetry in how they are arranged one-on-one. Well, crowns show the same thing. When you look down, you can begin to see the symmetry in the arrangement of the branches."

Reaching these treetops is a matter of climbing hand over hand up one of several 13-story-high TV towers. Once there, researchers can walk from one tower to another. Dr. Hinckley describes the ascent: "You begin in an area of mostly stemwood with a few small understory trees. As you go up, you see a branch and then a lot more branches and then you are no longer aware of the stemwood. You are more aware of crowns. At some point you begin to emerge and you are seeing trees some distance away. But you still have a tree crown right next to you. Literally your elbows are touching branches of a tree. You reach the apex of the tree and the sky is completely around you and you are above everything. It's like being a bird."

UNTIL 1970 DOUGLAS FIR was the only native conifer in British Columbia whose complete reproductive cycle had been chronicled. Now, with the help of the scanning electron micrograph, the curtain has been lifted on the innermost procreative efforts of other commercially important conifer species, which resemble that of Douglas fir.

Because I live among Douglas fir I have observed its reproductive effort as it unfolds over 17 months. In any month I can tune in on two overlapping cycles – the beginning stages of this year's and the conclusion of last year's – and see the start of bud development, the dispersal of pollen, flowering, flushing (a burst of vegetation), and the growth of both pollen and seed cones.

By the first of April Douglas fir's winter dormancy has come to an end. At the tip of each twig is a reddish-brown pointed bud, scale-covered, and about half an inch long. It is a hallmark of Douglas fir, separating the species from the true firs. Inside it are all the parts of a new branch or an extension to the existing branch. In April, as I wait for something to happen externally, rudimentary new buds for next year – bud primordia – are beginning to form within the vegetative bud. In May this vegetative bud will burst out of its scales and soft, light green pom-poms of foliage will decorate the tips of branches.

Although the bud primordia aren't visible at this time, they are beginning to develop. Over the next two months, as the shoot elongates, the new buds decide what they will be the following year – seed cones, pollen cones, or vegetative buds – and by early July become visible. A new vegetative bud sits at the tip of the branch. Near it is a seed-cone bud and farther down the twig are pollen-cone buds. There is also a backup – a latent bud that will develop into a new shoot if the terminal bud is removed. By early summer a scanning electron micrograph would show the rudimentary forms of leaves, pollen, or bracts (which overlap each scale), all arranged spirally on an axis. It is because of this spiral arrangement that the biological term for a cone is strobilus, coming from the Greek *strobilos* – a twisted object. While no change can be seen externally, the buds continue to develop internally until October or November and become dormant in December.

The second spring of the cycle is as dramatic and sexy as it gets. Nothing seems to be happening in March, but the seed and pollen cones formed last year are growing inside their scales. Through the process of meiosis, mother cells in the male bud divide into microspores, which have a haploid or half-number of chromosomes. The microspores develop wings and are called pollen grains. Inside the female cone, on the upper surface of each scale, is the ovule with mother cells, which divide into megaspores, again with half the requisite number of chromosomes.

About April 1 my trees start to rain down a yellow dust. At the same time the trees display narrow, bushy female flowers. The ones I see are auburn, but Douglas fir expert Jack Woods, at the B.C. Forest Service, tells me the species produces "a wonderful and subtle range of color that can only be appreciated by a geneticist who has spent too many hours breeding them. Colors range from lime-green to bright burgundy-red. Some have a mix of color such as red with green inner veins."

The pendant male cones shed their pollen, borne by the wind to the females, which for a tremulous week or so sit upright and receptive on their branches. The pollen grains drift into their open scales and are propelled toward the two ovules at the base of each scale. When the pollen reaches the ovules, the scales and bracts of the cone quickly close. Fertilization isn't accomplished until late May when the nuclei of the male and female cells fuse, doubling the number of chromosomes. The fertilized eggs form an embryonic plant covered with a seed coat and a seed wing.

Outwardly I see the seed cones elongate and hang down. Throughout this second July they are green and coated with a sticky, sugary-looking substance. By late August they turn brown. Usually in September, when a specialized tissue at the base of the scales dries out, the cone opens and the tiny seeds are released and carried on their wings a distance away from their towering parent.

Most of the giant conifers we are profiling follow this reproductive pattern over roughly the same length of time – from 15 to 17 months – although yellow cedar requires 28 months. Douglas firs are able to produce cones beginning at age 20 to 25. Some individual western red cedars, western hemlocks, or silver firs may not be sexually reproductive until they are 30, but the tree that beats them all is the grand fir, which must wait until it is 50 before beginning to produce seed.

Most conifers are monoecious – they have male and female flowers on the same tree – which raises the issue of self-pollination, known to breeders as "selfing." Conifers have developed ways to prevent this. The female flowers may be above male cones on the branch or in the crown so that self-pollen is less likely to enter them, or the two may reach maturity at a slightly different time. If pollen from the same tree and another tree enter the flower, it seems likely that the self-pollen would be slower in growing its penetrating pollen tube. If self-fertilization does occur, the female cone may abort or the seeds may be empty. If a self-fertilized seed germinates, the seedling may show abnormalities. It is interesting, however, that western red cedar successfully self-pollinates, having purged itself of most of these mechanisms.

Western red cedar is also the most prolific producer of seeds: between 227,000 and 590,000 to a pound. But when the larger numbers are reached, a great proportion will be small, flat, empty, or damaged by insects. By comparison Pacific silver fir produces between 7,800 and 20,800 seeds per pound.

It is March as I write this, and as usual nothing seems to be happening out there with the Douglas firs. But by April Fools' Day, I know, my car and decks will again be golden with pollen from my procreating conifers.

Western hemlock is a prodigious producer of small seed cones, which are easy to find on the ground.

A Great Host Bigleaf Maple

IN 1980 NALINI NADKARNI climbed a rope into the crown of a bigleaf maple in a Washington rainforest and made a discovery about this tree and its mossy companions that changed ideas long held by earthbound botanists. Dr. Nadkarni, now an ecologist on the faculty of Evergreen State College in Olympia, Washington, is considered one of the pioneering elite of canopy researchers – a scientist whose unearthing of treetop marvels made the cover of *Science*, and a wife and mother who was photographed at work in Costa Rica and featured as "Tree Woman" by *Glamour* magazine.

As a doctoral student at the University of Washington in Seattle, Nadkarni convinced her graduate committee that studying life in the treetops was key to understanding forest ecology. She proposed to compare the ecological roles of canopy plants in a Washington rainforest with those of a cloud forest in Costa Rica. The old-growth rainforests on the Olympic Peninsula resemble tropical rainforests in that their trees are covered with epiphytes – plants such as mosses and lichens. Although epiphytes may seem to be parasites, they merely use the tree as a place to park, taking their moisture and nutrients from air and rain. All the trees in the Olympic's Hoh River valley, primarily massive Sitka spruce and western hemlock, support epiphytes – overall, 130 species of lichens, liverworts, mosses, and ferns. But the tree that has the most, perhaps because of chemicals in its bark, is bigleaf maple.

In a grove of maples, known as the Hall of Mosses, visitors enter an exquisite hanging garden. *Selaginella oregana*, a club moss closer to a fern because it has a system of veins, trails off trees in six-foot-long beards; *Lobaria oregana*, commonly called lettuce lung, is a lime-colored, leafy lichen, which fixes nitrogen, and when it falls from the tree, fertilizes the soil or provides a pickup salad for elk and deer; *Polypodium glycyrrhiza*, considered the most important epiphytic fern in the Hoh, is known as the licorice fern because of the taste of its rhizome.

Today construction cranes give easier access to the treetops, but Dr. Nadkarni did her research when scientists ascended a rope that

Living on nutrients in air and rain, mosses and lichens park themselves on bigleaf maple hosts such as these on Vancouver Island.

had been shot over a limb with a crossbow, inching themselves up with the help of mountaineering equipment. For two years she climbed trees and clipped epiphytes, taking them back to her lab to be dried, weighed, and assessed. Using several bigleaf maples, Nadkarni calculated that the amount of plant material in the epiphytes was four times greater than the foliage of the host trees. The epiphytes concealed a thick mat of humus or true soil, and the combined weight of plants and soil on average in each tree was about 94 pounds. This material, of course, weighs a great deal more when soaked with rain, a burden to which the tree has gradually accommodated itself.

Nadkarni's great discovery in the treetops, which she herself describes as "frontier science," came when she rolled these mats back and found roots – lengthy roots that came from the bigleaf's own branches and trunk. Contrary to long-held belief, the tree was getting something from its lodgers, taking rent in the form of nutrients from the epiphytes it was housing. The discovery helped explain how sufficient nutrients are supplied to trees growing on soil often leached by rain.

Together the epiphyte-supporting trees and the nutrient-catching epiphytes contribute to their ecosystem by holding nutrients that might be lost. During the winter, when the maple host is leafless and incapable of extracting mineral ions from heavy rainfalls, its epiphytes are growing and intercepting these aerial-borne nutrients. In dry weather the organic matter under living epiphytic mosses and liverworts stays moist, which maintains a nutrient supply. The tree is most active in taking up nutrients in the summer when the epiphytes are drying and browning; in winter when it is leafless, the epiphytes take over. As well, the leaves and litter from bigleaf maples are high in potassium, calcium, and other nutrients, which build the soil when the leaves decay. And so between them, the maples and their penthouse pals cooperate in adding to the mineral capital of their ecosystem.

AS AN EX-EASTERNER accustomed to the symmetrical crowns of city-grown sugar and red maples with their brilliant autumn reds, yellows, and oranges, I was incredulous when a realtor pointed to "that maple there." Some sort of West Coast delusion, I thought, as I looked at the tree he was indicating. This monster, with great vertical stems, all burly and moss-covered, couldn't be a maple. But, of course, it was. *Acer macrophyllum.* Of the more than 100 species of the genus worldwide, this is the one with the big leaves. And that is no West Coast exaggeration. One day last October, when the leaves

OPPOSITE
Often bigger than a dinner plate, the leaves of a bigleaf maple can be up to two feet wide.

FOLLOWING PAGES
With trunks up to 37 feet in circumference and 100 feet tall, the West Coast's bigleaf maples have no problem qualifying as giants. This majestic individual is found near Deroche, British Columbia.

had turned yellow and were lying on the ground, I brought a fine example home. At its widest point it measured 15 inches – five inches bigger than a dinner plate, but small compared to the two-foot-wide leaves reported in the University of Washington's *Arboretum Bulletin*. The leaves have five deeply notched lobes.

Bigleaf maple is always found within 180 miles of the Pacific. Its continuous coast range begins near the northern end of Vancouver Island and ends near San Francisco. Isolated groves extend the coast range into San Diego County. Inland it grows on the western slopes of the Sierra Nevada as far south as Sequoia National Park.

An attractive feature of this tree is the way each of its large leaves finds a place in the light, seemingly without overlapping a neighbor. In the summertime, in our predominantly conifer forests, bigleaf maples are islands of cheery, dappled light and near-transluscent leaves, turning on their long stalks to present themselves face up to the sun. The stalks, by the way, are unusual among maples in that cutting them produces a milky sap. And speaking of sap, bigleaf maples can be tapped to make maple syrup.

The bigleafs I see in the forest where I live aren't massive; they run more to height, each tree having several great, mounting, 100-foot-high stems. But the champion specimens in Oregon, Washington, and British Columbia, which are also about 100 feet high, do have massive trunks, measuring respectively 37, 33, and 35 feet in circumference. The crowns of forest-grown trees are narrow, while open-grown trees have short trunks, which soon divide into large limbs that spread to support a pleasing broad, round crown.

Two hundred is a senior age for bigleaf maple. At 10 the tree is sexually mature. It is polygamous, having flowers that are either male, with a stamen only, or perfect, with both stamen and pistils. These tiny, greenish-yellow, scented flowers hang down in long clusters, which appear before the leaves in March and attract insects that helpfully distribute the pollen. The fruit is the familiar key – a seed in a case with an attached wing, known as a samara. As do others of the genus, bigleaf maple produces a double samara – two joined keys. The oversized seeds, three-quarters of an inch long, are in a seed case, which is unusual in having a hairy, rough-to-touch covering. The samaras hang on the tree in clusters, and when the seeds have matured in the fall, many of the keys will detach themselves from the tree in a breeze and gyrate to the ground in a spiral flight, which slows their descent and allows them to travel a distance away from their parent.

Not a great deal of scientific work has been done on the regeneration of bigleaf maple from seeds. It is known that the seeds germinate

Long beards of club moss trail off bigleaf maples in the Hall of Mosses in the Hoh River valley on the Olympic Peninsula.

in January or February and do well on mineral soil and organic substrates, but life for the seedlings is hazardous. Researchers in Oregon followed the progress of naturally regenerated seedlings and sown seeds in two of Oregon State University's forests. They found that bigleaf maples must slip into the forest succession at the right time. In a clearcut every single seedling will be mowed down by rodents and deer. In among Douglas firs they have a better chance, especially if they begin life when the conifers have begun to slough off their lower branches and light is being admitted into the stand. Later in the succession, when the older Douglas firs are losing their upper branches and more light has created an understory of shrubs and small plants, maple seedlings will not get started. Given the perils of regeneration by seedlings, it is a good thing that bigleaf maples sprout profusely. As many as 67 sprouts have been counted on a single stump, and in five years these trees have reached heights of 17 feet.

Bigleaf maple is another among the few broad-leaved trees on the coast to have been commercially harvested. Sold in a mix with other maples as western soft maple, it is said to be suitable for domestic flooring, furniture, piano actions, sports equipment, and paneling. Because of its strength, bigleaf maple forms the back, sides, and necks of violins, bass fiddles, and guitars.

Some trees have a curly grain that makes their wood particularly valuable. It is sought commercially to make a decorative face veneer. But it is also what professional musicians want to see on the backs of their electric guitars and are willing to pay for. Reid Hudson, a Vancouver Islander who supplies wood to instrument makers, tells of a man who, in 1986, bought an enormous bigleaf maple for $100. It was six feet in diameter and its wood was solid to its center. Over the next four years he sold the wood for $40,000. "If it had been seasoned wood," Hudson says, "he would have got $100,000." Hudson himself was one of the buyers, purchasing three truckloads and going back in 1990 for the last few small pieces, which he sold to a manufacturer in the Philippines for $15,000. Lamenting that he has never found another tree like that, he seeks out what is available in Oregon, Washington, British Columbia's Fraser Valley, and on the east coast of Vancouver Island. Because trees from wetter locations are rotten in the center, he looks for those that grew in the open where air circulation seems to prevent rot. Maples produce several figures in their wood – among them a bird's eye, which is caused by localized indentations of the annual growth rings, and a quilted pattern that results when the growth rings are crowded and form elongated bulges. The curly pattern runs at right angles to the growth

120

———

GIANTS

rings and is the result of undulations in the rings. When the waves – or flames, as Hudson calls them – run across widely spaced and pronounced annual rings, the effect resembles a plaid shirt, at least in the opinion of a luthier who refuses to use the wood. Most instrument makers, though, do like the curly grain, particularly if it can be found in the wood of a tree that grew slowly so that its annual rings are close together. Curly grain doesn't begin to develop until a tree is two feet in diameter, and it occurs closer to the bark than to the center of the tree and closer to the bottom of the tree than to the top. Knowing this you can tell by looking at the back of a guitar how the wood was oriented in the tree. With age the pattern extends farther into the heartwood, and so big-diameter trees are esteemed for the backs of big instruments. The curly pattern occurs in only a small proportion of trees and may be genetically influenced. Reid Hudson has a friend who is banking on this possibility. He has taken cuttings from bigleaf maples with the pattern and has planted them on two acres of land. "It's a 75-year turnaround and a gamble," Hudson says, "but he's planning to leave them for his grandchildren."

John Bese has a slightly different interest in bigleaf maple. He is a member of the Fraser Valley Wood Turners' Guild and a teacher of wood turning to hobbyists. His specialty is turning maple burls, as large as three feet wide and a foot thick, on an industrial lathe to make bowls or platters. "Burl grain runs in swirls. It looks like half a cloud or big popcorn," he tells me. Then he adds modestly for someone whose work appears in juried shows, "The art is already in the wood. You have to bring it out." Bese says he would never cut a tree unless it is a hazard, and so his burls come from blow-downs. But with the demand in the United States and Taiwan for Canadian bigleaf maple, he is having a harder time finding the wood he needs. In Taiwan, he explained, bigleaf maple burls are delicately sliced to a super-thin veneer, which is applied to plywood and shipped back to North America to be sold for expensive paneling.

Even though its size makes it unsuitable for urban gardens, landscape architects praise the bigleaf maple in the right settings. Cornelia Oberlander, Canada's preeminent landscape architect – responsible for the landscaping of the National Gallery of Canada in Ottawa and the Canadian embassy in Washington – maintains a wild bigleaf maple in a ravine behind her Vancouver house. She prunes it every spring to free the trunk of branchy growth so that she can see the bark, which she finds so interesting. "It is one of the most wonderful trees because of its bark and its leaves," she says, "which in the fall turn a wonderful gold in contrast to the green of the conifers." In a recent environmentally responsible landscaping project at the University of British Columbia, she cleared away existing vegetation but kept all the bigleaf maples. "You've come to the right person," she adds. "I think it's a wonderful tree." Nor is she alone in her enthusiasm. Seattle landscape architect Arthur Kruckeberg points out that elsewhere in the world the bigleaf is considered the noblest of maples. "Overwhelmingly majestic," he writes, "a tree of great beauty."

ABOUT MID-FEBRUARY I can discern a pinkish haze in the crowns of stands of red alder at sea level on the coast. After a winter that has not been long, cold, and bitter as elsewhere, but dark, wet, and depressing, the pinking of the red alders is still a welcome first faint promise that the forest trees are bestirring themselves. In a few weeks caterpillarlike catkins will release their pollen, which will waft about unmercifully, and the season of Seldane will have begun. But this year I will take my medicine without cursing this prolific broad-leaved tree. Instead I am going to picture the alders contributing bags and bags of fertilizer to the earth.

Red alder (*Alnus rubra*) is also known as Oregon alder, western alder, and Pacific coast alder. It is the largest of the 30 *Alnus* species around the world, eight of which grow in North America. The species' range is from southeastern Alaska to southern California in a narrow lowland strip along the coast, usually within 125 miles of the ocean. The most plentiful broad-leaved tree on the coast, it is also the most commercially important, growing rapidly when it is young and achieving heights of around 80 feet in 75 years.

There seem to be a number of explanations for the common name red alder. En masse and from a distance the male catkins give the tree a red blush (a deepening, I suppose, of the pink haze I have seen). The bark of freshly cut trees appears red, and aboriginal peoples derived a red dye from the inner bark, which made their nets invisible to fish. The wood turns reddish after it is cut. That feature, common in alders, was equated with blood by superstitious early Europeans, who decided the tree was a symbol of evil.

Lumbermen on the coast may not have held that superstition, but they were prejudiced against red alder. Thirty years ago, when I first moved to the coast and bought a house with an alder planted in the front yard, I heard all the negative clichés about this tree. It was a weed, it would be rotten at its heart in eight years, it would grow tall and thin and be a danger to us all. In time, when the tree got to be excessively tall and was leaning south toward our house, we cut it down and discovered we had acquired quite a bit of sound wood, which the following winter provided some lovely evenings in front of the fireplace.

But out in the forest every effort was being made to get rid of this tree, which sprang up so promptly in cutover areas. Red alder grew easily, as B.C. logger-poet Pete Trower wrote, "rising like an ambush on raked ridges," dominating the light-dependent Douglas fir, which was the tree of economic desire. Once again, being a culture in a hurry to make a buck, we missed the lesson that nature was trying to teach. It was through happenstance that silviculturists in Oregon began to learn what would happen if red alders were left to mix it up with Douglas firs.

Robert F. Tarrant was a director of the Pacific Northwest Forest and Range Experiment Station of the USDA Forest Service in Portland. He tells of discovering and spending a few hours in a plantation of red alder and Douglas fir in the Wind River Experimental Forest. It was a stand that had been planted with Douglas fir after a devastating fire in 1927, and a few years later, as an experiment, red alder seedlings were intermixed with the conifers. It was a hot day when Tarrant found the stand, but this plantation was several degrees cooler than the surrounding area of pure Douglas fir (a microclimate often found in mixed stands). The Douglas firs growing with the alder had very dark green foliage, with more and larger needles. The conifers were bigger and in better form than those outside the plantation. A later survey estimated the total production of wood on the site had been doubled.

Those Douglas firs were benefiting from the red alder's ability to improve the fertility of the soil. Alder has root nodules, like those of legumes, which fix atmospheric nitrogen and make it available to the soil, either by excreting it directly or through the decomposition of roots, nodules, and leaf litter. Alder may contribute hundreds of pounds of nitrogen to an acre, adding even more if the soil was initially depleted. (Ironically silviculturists who had assiduously removed red alders experimented with nitrogen fertilizers in Douglas fir plantations.) The alder also enriches the soil with organic matter.

Silviculturists took up the red alder banner about two decades ago, and their appreciation for it increases. Because it grows rapidly and fixes nitrogen, they have planted it experimentally with Douglas fir and black cottonwood on problem sites, such as coal mine spoils, landslides, erosions, and in areas where the soil is low in fertility. It now protects streambanks and roadsides and provides fire- and windbreaks. Planting a tree such as red alder and letting it grow for 40 or 50 years on a site infected with *Phellinus weiri* seems to be the only way to control this root pathogen, which kills conifers. In other experiments red alder foliage, twigs, and sawdust have been added to cattle feed. As a wood, it burns efficiently, makes pulp for tissues and writing paper, turns well on a lathe, and is admired by woodcarvers and furniture-makers for its ability to take and hold a stain.

Pete Trower caught the essence of the trees in his poem "The

Alders." He called them the "reoccupiers," the "encroachers," "the forestfixers bandaging brown wounds with applegreen sashes." We make the wounds and nature tries to heal them. It took time, but we have acknowledged that red alder is a remedy, not an enemy.

Now appreciated for its ability to fix nitrogen in the soil, red alder grows in lowland areas with companions such as skunk cabbage.

IF TREES HAVE GENDER AND PERSONALITY, western hemlock is a woman who loves crowds, wears a flared and flouncing dancing dress that gives her an appearance of disarray, and hangs her head shyly in the shadows but is capable of taking over her domain and dominating it forever. She has a way of attracting champions, and so, despite her demure look, she is never to be underestimated.

A significant chapter in the biography of this deceptive tree begins in Prague in 1938, where the man who was to push it up the forest ladder of success was head of the sales department of the Czechoslovakian State Forests and a principal in a family lumber company founded 200 years earlier. Leon Koerner was a practical man. A former logger and sawmiller, he was an exporter of European softwoods and hardwoods and an executive of international timber organizations. When Germany occupied Czechoslovakia in October 1938, Koerner and his three brothers fled the country. In early 1939, after a stopover in London, Leon and his wife came to British Columbia and, by June 1939, he had formed a new lumber company in which his brothers soon joined him.

The Koerners decided to specialize in selling western hemlock to Britain, but they were faced with performing a makeover on a lady whose reputation had been destroyed by provincial sawmillers who had refused to alter their methods of producing lumber to suit British importers. An article published in London in 1940 described how western hemlock was perceived before the arrival of Leon Koerner: "Cut . . . on crude machines of up-country forest mills, using thick saws with wolflike fangs for teeth, miscut and often with ends that look as if the beaver had eaten its way for cross-cut, shipped almost green, can it be wondered it often presented an inglorious, discoloured, and shaken spectacle on arrival over here?"

The Koerners' first step was to rename the product using an old coastal synonym that had dropped out of use. With the blessing of the province's Chief Forester, F. C. Manning, who said, "I don't care what you call the wood if you can sell it," western hemlock became the sexier-sounding Alaska pine, and the Alaska Pine Co., Ltd. began production in July 1939 at a refitted sawmill in New Westminster on British

The western hemlock, Washington's state tree and the most plentiful tree in British Columbia, is able to grow demurely in the shadow of Douglas firs, waiting for the chance to spurt upward and dominate the forest.

Columbia's Lower Mainland. The Koerners bought their logs on the open market and prepared kiln- and air-dried lumber, properly sized for the European market. Each board was stamped with their trademark. A London magazine, *Timber and Plywood*, advised British buyers of good wood to inspect "Alaska pine shelvings and floorings which we saw a few weeks ago at the Surrey Commercial Docks. They are equal to any first class Swedish manufacture."

Western hemlock, AKA Alaska pine, sold well in the United Kingdom. Here on the West Coast during the Second World War, with the demand for Sitka spruce for airplanes and Douglas fir for pontoon bridges, soldiers' footlockers, and prefabricated barracks, western hemlock was increasingly cut for pulp. It had been discovered in the 1930s that the tree was as good a source as Sitka spruce for alpha cellulose, the alkali-resistant wood fiber needed to make paper. Its light-colored, nonresinous wood was an advantage in the sulphite and groundwood pulping processes then in use. Later, when kraft pulping and bleaching were introduced, western hemlock's qualities became irrelevant, and all softwoods were fed into the digesters. But hemlock remained the main source of wood fiber for the manufacture of cellophane, plastics, and rayon yarn. The dancing lady of the forest was converted to ball gowns and buttons, candy wrappers, steering wheels, and photographic film. The Koerners renamed their company Alaska Pine and Cellulose Ltd. and made it British Columbia's biggest producer of wood pulp for textiles. In 1954, when Leon Koerner retired, Rayonier Corporation of New York bought an 80 percent interest in the company and brother Walter became chairman of Rayonier Canada.

The Koerners had come to the best place on the coast for an enterprise based on western hemlock. It was then and still is the most plentiful tree in the seaboard forests of British Columbia, and (although this is Washington's state tree) the province possesses more of the species than Washington, Oregon, California, and Alaska combined. Not remotely related to the poison taken by Socrates, which came from an herb in the carrot family, hemlocks are members of the pine family. Their genus name, *Tsuga*, is a word that comes from the Japanese for hemlock – *Tsunga*. There are about 10 species worldwide. The two on the Pacific coast are western hemlock and mountain hemlock. Like hemlocks everywhere, they can be identified from a distance by their hung-over leading shoot, which bends away from the wind. While the mountain species has longer needles and distinctly longer cones, the first clue to distinguishing between the two trees is their habitat: a hemlock in a coastal forest is more likely to be western hemlock, one at subalpine elevations is more likely to be a mountain hemlock.

Western hemlock is the larger of the two species, reaching 150 to 200 feet. It seldom lives longer than 400 or 500 years, but a tree 700 years old was found in the Queen Charlotte Islands. Its specific epithet – *heterophylla* – means "different leaves," and an examination of a twig reveals blunt-tipped needles of two lengths. The longer ones, in two rows along the side, combined with the shorter ones sticking up along the top create an impression of disorderliness, or perhaps unpredictability. The leafy branchlets are held downward and spread out to receive light, forming graceful fans of greenery around the tree. On the underside of the fan the leaves present a silvery appearance because of lines of breathing pores – the stomata – on either side of a midvein. The tree produces many small seed cones, less than an inch long, and spent, brown cones are easy to find on the tree or on the ground below.

The best stands of western hemlock grow in the mild, humid climate of the foggy, rainy coast where the species finds the conditions to form what foresters call a climax forest – one in which the dominant tree goes on indefinitely replacing itself and is not succeeded by trees of another species. Forest succession is an ecosystem's evolving parade of plants, trees, and animals – a series of communities succeeded by new communities. If we consider only the trees, succession begins in a Pacific coast forest with red alder, which springs up quickly after a disturbance such as a fire or logging. It is part of what is called the pioneer community. In the next stage Douglas firs appear. These fast-growing conifers will soon be taller than the red alders, and in about 150 years, having attained a place at the head of the parade, will form a closed canopy, which will keep sunlight from the forest floor.

This isn't the ideal condition for Douglas fir regeneration. Its seeds may germinate if they can find the mineral soil they prefer, but as the seedlings grow a little older they need full sunlight to survive. Now it is western hemlock's turn to move in. The species is a prodigious producer of seed – eight million from an acre of 100-year-old trees was reported in Oregon – and the winged seed can travel a mile in a strong wind. Blown into a closed-canopy Douglas fir forest, the small seeds may settle on their preferred landing place – decaying logs or rotten wood – where they hope to find the moisture and nutrition they need. Well able to tolerate the shade that kills Douglas fir seedlings, the young western hemlocks can hang back in the understory, growing slowly and waiting for aging Douglas firs to lose their upper branches or to die. Blessed then by more light, the hemlocks will spurt up and dominate the stand by reproducing in their own shade and preventing the reintroduction of less-shade-tolerant trees.

The decaying stump of a Sitka spruce on the Olympic Peninsula has provided this western hemlock with a hospitable seedbed and given it a good start in life.

If nothing were to disturb a Pacific coast forest, and if many years passed, western hemlock would reign, either alone or with other shade-brooking trees such as western red cedar and Pacific silver fir. But in reality few forests escape fire, logging, or high winds – the kinds of disturbances that favor other species. Tall, older Douglas firs, which have a thicker bark than western hemlock, are more likely to survive a fire and will regenerate better when mineral soil has been bared by the burning off of organic debris. In a similar way clearcutting and slash-burning are intended to provide a beneficial environment for Douglas fir.

Once under way, western hemlock forests can be astonishingly dense. Foresters have counted 6,000 to 10,000 stems in an acre of 20-year-old naturally regenerated trees. If a western hemlock grows with some space around it, the tree retains its lower branches, but when many trees are close together, self-pruning produces narrower crowns. With trees thickly branched or closely packed, a stand of western hemlock feels dark, something that always strikes me when in the small forest around our island's main lake, I enter a gloomy pocket of western hemlock.

The species has been described as a supermarket for West Coast aboriginals, who scraped off the inner bark and cooked it fresh like pasta or dried it in cakes, which were later mixed with grease or salmon skins. The Haida considered cambium cakes with cranberries to be a feast treat for the gods. Branch tips added spice to other foods and fresh needles made a tea. The bark was used in dyeing and tanning leather.

Europeans, at first, were disdainful of the lady of the shady woods. She was associated with her cousin *Tsuga canadensis*, eastern hemlock, with its inferior wood. They left her uncut or tried to eliminate her as if she were a weed. In the 1940s and 1950s, she was dubbed a Cinderella and invited to the ball. After the war, technologists devised new ways for making and bleaching pulp, and western hemlock lost its status as the softwood of choice for pulping. By the mid-seventies lumber companies and foresters were again wondering how to manage a tree that had so many desirable characteristics: it was a prolific seeder and regenerated well in a variety of locations, survived in dense stands and grew well with other species, was relatively free of insects and disease when young, and produced a lot of wood. But the wood wasn't quite as desirable as Douglas fir – not as strong, not as easy to nail, not as easy to kiln-dry.

Today, it is known that on most scales devised for testing wood, western hemlock rates second only to Douglas fir. Because there is little difference between the heartwood and the sapwood, the wood is uniform in color. It wears well and hardens as it ages, which makes it a good alternative to hardwood flooring. The wood is odorless and pitch-free, a good choice as paneling for saunas. The general manager of a B.C. company, which employs 40 to 70 people a year in producing railings and spindles and other stair parts, says that western hemlock is one of the hardest softwoods, good for turning because it doesn't splinter, easy to finish because it has less resin. "Two- to 300-year-old trees, there couldn't be better wood," he told me. "British Columbia and Washington have the lion's share of the hemlock. The way God threw the seed – we were the lucky ones."

In the Hoh Rainforest on the Olympic Peninsula, I noticed western hemlocks with what appeared to be flared bases. The park ranger accompanying me explained that these trees had begun life on downed logs, sending their roots out and over the log, like a rider straddling a horse. Over time the log had decayed and the exposed roots grew in diameter, filling in the space where the log had been. Nurse logs are good seedbeds for western hemlock. At elevations where there is a winter snowpack, logs – by virtue of being the first surfaces to emerge from the snow – give western hemlock seedlings a slightly longer season to establish themselves. They also provide a more hospitable seedbed than the forest floor, which will have a thick mat of vegetation brought down in heavy snowfalls. Some observers report that a fully stocked stand of western hemlock can be made up of trees that have sent their roots into the soil around or through stumps or logs.

In mid-February I walked around our island lake to check out what had happened in the forest over the winter. A dramatic outcome of one of several hard windstorms was apparent on the northwest side of the lake. Lying parallel to the trail, as if placed by some tidy giant, were the trunks and green-leaved branches of several newly fallen trees. I clambered into the forest to view an upturned root disk and was able to reconstruct the tragedy. For whatever reason, the shallow roots of the most northerly tree had let go. In falling, this first tree, which had a trunk 40 inches wide, had brought down a second about 15 feet away, which in turn had brought down a third, which was about 120 feet tall. Three superior western hemlocks bowled over. Here, I thought, was a perfect example of the species' ecological weakness – shallow roots that make it vulnerable to windthrow. This triple play had been set up in the happy circumstance that gave the trees life. More than a century ago seeds had landed on a rotting log, and many seedlings had flourished along the trunk. Eventually three tall trees stood in a line that was just a memory of a nurse log long decayed. Now they were lying side by side, having succumbed to the line. But then I realized I was looking at three potential nurse logs for the seeds that will arrive here this year or next, and that the line would re-form.

THE ARBUTUS, OR MADRONE, is so outstanding in our coastal forests that I wonder how it escaped widespread plundering or silvicultural management. Perhaps the novelty and flamboyant beauty of this bark-shedding, copper-trunked tree have stayed the hand of the woodcutter, while its unpredictable growth and unreliable wood may have turned silviculturalists to more amenable species.

In the United States this Pacific coast tree is known as madrone (or madrona or madrono), a name it was given by a Spanish missionary, Father Juan Crespi, in 1769. In 1792 Archibald Menzies saw what he called "the Strawberry Tree" near Port Discovery, Washington, and his contribution in bringing it to the attention of the European botanical world is recognized in the scientific binomial – *Arbutus menziesii*. The genus *Arbutus*, of which there are 20 trees and shrubs worldwide, is part of the larger heath family along with rhododendrons, blueberries, heathers, and salal. The United States has Texas and Arizona madrone, but Canada's only *Arbutus* is the Pacific species, which Canadians commonly call arbutus. It is, as well, the country's only native broad-leaved evergreen.

A. menziesii, to use the term that crosses the border, ranges for 1,100 miles on the coast. Wrapping around the Strait of Georgia and Puget Sound and onto the islands of both those bodies of water, it continues as far south as Mount Palomar in San Diego County, California, and can also be found in the Sierra Nevada.

Although I have included the species because it is such an unusual and attractive feature of the coastal forests, it can be a tree of no mean stature. The tallest ever recorded, according to Arthur Lee Jacobson, author of *Trees of Seattle*, was 130 feet. The current American champion, in Humboldt County, California, is 96 feet tall and 34 feet in circumference (about double the girth of most very large specimens). British Columbia's reigning giant, which is much slimmer than the California tree, was measured at 104 feet in 1986 on Thetis, one of the Gulf Islands in the Strait of Georgia. Within hailing distance of Thetis is tiny Dayman, a privately owned island, where in 1993 I was shown the largest *A. menziesii* I had ever seen – a straight bole, undivided for 40 or 50 feet and with a crown that topped out at more than twice that height. The arbutus was in among conifers and away from the sunny, dry locations the species usually prefers. The tree grows particularly well in the drier climate of southern Vancouver Island and in and around the provincial capital of Victoria, where several heritage trees have been preserved. In one case a major road was divided and utility lines were buried to save a landmark tree.

Although *A. menziesii* is usually stately, the tree will respond to its location and produce twisted, bent, or leaning forms, which seem to be the result of its attempt to stay in the sun. It may have multiple stems, with one branching out and staying parallel to the ground until it finds a spot of light and turns upward. On a rocky outcrop where no other tree can cling, it will lean away from the slope into the light. I have a dozen arbutus on the east-facing rocky slope in front of my house. Today, as I write, they are being buffeted by a strong wind from the south, and I am grateful for the tree's habit of putting down deep and wide-spreading roots.

Watching my colony of arbutus, I have come to the conclusion that *A. menziesii* puts on the best show of all our Pacific coast trees. Even in winter, just by glowing like copper on a dull day, it provides relief from the ever-greenness of its conifer neighbors and the surrounding salal. Caught in the rays of a setting winter sun, it warms to a ruddy hue, a contrast to its shiny green, leathery leaves, which stay with it throughout the winter so that it never takes on the skeletal look of deciduous trees. In the spring *A. menziesii* rings a new change with its clusters of small, white, bell-shaped flowers, whose fragrance lures insects and hummingbirds. The flowers are what botanists call "perfect" – they are hermaphrodites with stamens and pistils in the same flower. Just after the flowers, new leaves appear – oval, glossy, leathery. Throughout this time the tree's thin, papery bark is cracking and peeling, like sunburned skin, to reveal a greenish, smooth-as-silk new bark underneath. About midsummer, when the white flowers have faded to yellow, the old leaves turn red and crisp and drop off. By September grapelike clusters of pea-sized, seed-containing, coral-red berries hang from branch tips, attracting birds, who supposedly get intoxicated by eating them in large quantities. The stomach of a California pigeon was found to contain 111 berries, enough to have prevented it from flying. Deer mice in the Sierra Nevada prefer the berry to peanut butter or wheat flakes, but most people find them inedible, a fact reflected in the name of the tree's European cousin, *Arbutus unedo* – Latin for "I eat one." In our mild climate, berries not picked off by deer, birds, and mice still decorate the trees in January.

Even though the mature trees produce a good quantity of seed, which germinates reasonably well, very few seedlings survive. They fall prey to slugs, fungi, and drought. If they do get established – and they are particular in needing bare mineral soil as a seedbed – they progress slowly. The species is much more efficient at reproducing by sprouting, either from dormant buds at the root collar or from cut stumps. As many as 300 sprouts were counted on one such stump. These sprouts grow rapidly, reaching heights of 10 feet in three years.

The cherry-colored wood, which seems as though it should be sought out by carvers and craftsmen, is hard and tends to warp and check as it dries. It has been used for flooring, furniture, paneling, and such novelties as tobacco pipes – and Californians once preferred to make gunpowder with madrone charcoal.

The European arbutus failed to inspire a tradition of folklore; the Pacific tree has a few aboriginal associations. Some Native peoples boiled the leaves, bark, and roots to make a cure for colds or sore throats. In California they are said to have venerated the tree and selected one isolated individual in southwestern Humboldt County as a location for coast and interior tribes to meet and make treaties.

Today's gardener who wants to tame this wild tree may have difficulty transplanting it but much less trouble maintaining it, except for the endless litter of bark and foliage. As Arthur Kruckeberg writes in *Gardening with Native Plants in the Pacific Northwest*, "The daring gardener with little space should chance a smallish specimen in a starved sunny corner where it will not make too rampant a growth. Indeed, the madrone thrives on neglect. Give it a dryish, exposed piece of the garden and it will take care of itself, once established."

On a rocky outcrop on Galiano Island, British Columbia, an eternally showy arbutus, or madrone, reaches for the sun.

The Friendly Giant Sitka Spruce

HARNESSED AND LINKED TO ROPES, Richard Ring waits to be pulled up into the canopy of a Sitka spruce. He is in the Carmanah Valley, an old-growth forest on the southwest side of Vancouver Island, where environmentalists have counted 239 Sitka spruce more than 230 feet tall. One of these trees became familiar to British Columbians as the poster symbol in the successful struggle to save the ancient valley where this species, *Picea sitchensis*, has achieved a magnificent maturity. The Carmanah Giant – a 314-foot-high tower, the world's tallest Sitka spruce – was accurately measured by dropping a plumb line from the top. It is not the *biggest*, however. Just across Juan de Fuca Strait, in Washington's Olympic National Park, there is a shorter but much wider Sitka spruce. Only 191 feet tall, the American – and likely world – champion has a diameter of 19 feet, which is wider than the rooms most of us occupy (see "Tracking Down the Record Trees," page 9).

In British Columbia's Upper Carmanah Valley a researcher is pulled to the top of a Sitka spruce. University of Victoria entomologists have found more than 1,300 species of canopy-dwelling insects.

The size of the tree is not what fascinates Richard Ring. Faculty entomologist at the University of Victoria and president of the Entomological Society of Canada, Dr. Ring is one shoot of that burgeoning branch of science, forest canopy research. Driving from the university this spring day, he has traveled for four hours, part of it along a rough road no longer maintained by the logging company that once hoped to cut the trees here. An hour's walk into the rainforest brings him to a research station set up by Western Canada Wilderness Committee environmentalists who five years ago had the bright idea that attracting scientists into the forest might help save it. Around him are the awesome results of a windstorm in February 1995: a dozen trees, 30 inches in diameter, are down, two lying in a providential V around the building where researchers sleep and cook. Their shallow roots have been wrenched out of the ground.

But the five giant Sitka spruce chosen for canopy research have survived. As two climbing assistants, one on the ground and one in the branches 125 feet above, begin to haul on the ropes, Ring concentrates on the tree in front of him, focusing on the fantastic patterns he sees in the bark. For what seems like 10 minutes, but might be only five, he rises. If this were an elevator in an office tower, he would be at the 11th floor when the ascent ends. He is helped onto a small platform attached to the tree with canvas straps. Immediately he feels safe in the welcoming branches; he can't see the ground. Around him all is luxuriant greenness. The tops of the branches are covered with mosses, and in a well-developed layer of soil, tree seedlings, ferns, and salal are growing. In the uppermost canopy there are plants with little white flowers. "It's another world," he says.

In the Pacific Northwest, Sitka spruce ranges from Mendocino County in California, through Oregon, Washington, British Columbia (including the isolated Queen Charlotte Islands), and Alaska. Unlike other trees on the Pacific coast, Sitka spruce grow in higher elevations in the north than they do in the south. California's Sitka spruce are at the mouths of streams and in low valleys facing the Pacific, but in British Columbia the tree has been found at 5,000 feet. In Alaska dwarf specimens tough it out at 3,900 feet on unglaciated rocky outcrops above the Juneau Icefield. The aged giants, however, endure closer to the sea: on the west coast of Vancouver Island they abide in the Carmanah, Walbran, and Khutzeymateen valleys, and in Clayoquot Sound. In Washington state the great Sitkas are in the Hoh, Queets, and Quinault valleys of Olympic National Park.

The Carmanah Giant and the other record-making individuals of this long-lived, fast-growing species have been beneficially bathed in sea spray. Unlike other conifers, Sitka spruce tolerate the salt and can extract other minerals from the spray. Their blue-green needles absorb phosphorus, as well as calcium and magnesium, which the tree requires in large quantities.

The Hoh River valley in Washington is a great place to see Sitka spruce. On the road into the national park portion of the valley, I stopped to admire "the Big Spruce," which, at 270 feet, is one of the loftiest on the Olympic Peninsula. Sitka spruce is the dominant tree in the Hoh rainforest where it is able to attain large sizes because fog reaches 30 miles into the valley from the coast. As park ranger Mary Dessel told me, without the fog there wouldn't be Sitka spruce in this forest. With the high rainfall in the Hoh, 300-foot-tall trees need roots that go only five feet into the ground. As a result, windthrow is Sitka spruce's main undoing. "This past March," Dessel said, "there were winds of 80 miles an hour. Trees were coming down like crazy, sounding like a thunderstorm."

Dessel showed me a Sitka spruce that had dropped in the March storm, and later on the trail, we walked beside a 190-foot individual

*Sitka spruce needles surround the twig like a
bottlebrush and are painfully sharp to the touch.*

that had fallen perhaps a decade before. "You can think of downed logs as savings accounts of nutrients for the forest," she said. The tree that fell this year had been immediately attacked by ambrosia beetles. It takes these beetles as little as two days to bore tunnels into a newly downed tree. They don't eat wood but grow their own food – fungus farms, which they start by depositing fungal spores they carry in a little pouch called a mycangia. The early scavengers – carbohydrate-eating fungi, bacteria, and insects – are followed by fungi that decompose the cellulose and lignin of the sapwood. Fungi are introduced into the wood by many kinds of beetles, which pick them up as they walk through the forest. A final stage in decomposition is the attack on the heartwood by brown cubical rot, which absorbs the white cellulose but not the brown lignin, turning the wood red and separating it into chunks. The long process of decay may take 300 or 400 years for a huge Douglas fir but only a century for Sitka spruce and western hemlock of equal sizes.

Downed logs, with their open areas and stores of nutrients, offer the seedlings of some trees a good place to get started in life. Since Douglas fir prefers mineral soil as a seedbed and western red cedar usually does, too, it is Sitka spruce and western hemlock whose seeds germinate on a nurse log. In the Hoh forest, elk love to eat western hemlock seedlings from the logs, and so it is often only Sitka spruce that remains. The seedlings that survive the competition for space and light and aren't sloughed off when decayed bark falls can survive for many years on the nourishment provided by the log, but only those that get their roots into mineral soil will grow into mature trees. When the nurse log has rotted away, Sitka spruce may have thick, aboveground roots with a hollow space in the center, a reminder of the log they once straddled.

Dessel agreed that it can be difficult to identify conifers, especially in an old-growth forest where the bark is covered with moss, the leaves are out of reach in the canopy, and the cones have been carried away by rodents. Earlier I had been with a forester who identified a conifer by shaking hands with a leaf-covered twig. "Ouch," he said. "That's a spruce." Sitka spruce needles are stiff and sharp, painful to touch, and surround the branch like a bristly bottlebrush. You cannot roll them between your fingers. Dark green on the top, the needles have whitish bands underneath. The two- to four-inch-long pendant cones have thin, papery scales with ragged margins. In deep forests, where the lower trunks are bare of branches, bark is a good clue to Sitka spruce. Scaly rather than ridged, it is purplish or reddish-brown. The round scales break off easily, revealing a lighter-colored new bark underneath.

Picea sitchensis has a special relationship with Alaska. It is the official state tree and was named for Sitka Island (now Baranof Island), the site in southeastern Alaska of the Russian-American Company's first permanent settlement in North America. The tree grows around the Gulf of Alaska from Ketchikan – the gateway to Misty Fjords National Monument where 2.3 million acres of spruce, hemlock, and cedar forests are protected – to Kodiak Island where there are pure stands of Sitka spruce. The 17-million-acre Tongass National Forest, of which Misty Fjords is a part, and the four-million-acre Chugach National Forest have been the sources of most of the Sitka logged in the state.

Sitka spruce grew abundantly on Baranof Island in the Russian period, but out on the Aleutians life was treeless and bleak. Hoping to make the islands more habitable, the Russians planted wildlings on three small islands in Unalaska Bay. The exact year of the first planting is uncertain, but whether it was 1805 or 1807, the Sitka spruce on Amaknak Island are the oldest commercial forest plantation in North America. Because of grazing animals and fire, only three trees survive, endowed with historical landmark status.

America's smallest national forest also grew out of a desire to make life more pleasant in the Aleutian Islands. During World War II, when the islands were occupied by military personnel, tree planting was seen as a way to boost morale. In 1942, 10,000 spruce seedlings were planted near Fort Glenn on Umnak Island, and in 1944, 50 spruce were set out on Adak Island, encased in burlap bag shelters. By 1964 these trees had grown to heights of four to 12 feet and the area was declared a national forest, for which one economical sign was erected: YOU ARE NOW ENTERING AND LEAVING ADAK NATIONAL FOREST.

In the two world wars, Sitka spruce suffered high casualties. The wood has the highest strength-to-weight ratio of any wood and can absorb shock better than metal. It is easy to repair, too: you can plug a bullet hole with plastic wood or saw up some new bits and replace the injured part. In World War I the U.S. Army had a Spruce Division, 10,000 soldiers logging on the Pacific coast from Juan de Fuca Strait to California, producing millions of board feet of Sitka spruce to build airplanes. To meet Great Britain's needs, B.C. sawmills were kept in full production processing the spruce, much of it logged from the Queen Charlotte Islands.

In World War II the highest-quality, knot-free Alaska Sitka spruce was towed to Puget Sound in rafts of a million board feet to construct airplanes. B.C. spruce was drafted for the famous Mosquito, the speedy bomber that could drop a load of 4,000-pounders and elude pursuing Luftwaffe fighters. Almost 8,000 Mosquitoes were built in Britain, Australia, and Downsview, Ontario. In Britain skilled furniture craftsmen, rather than metalworkers, were hired by de Havilland, the company that designed and manufactured the plane. They used spruce where strength was needed – at the edges of doors, at the wing attachments, on the joint between the halves of the fuselage, and as stringers between the upper and lower skins of the wing. In 1944 nearly 342 million board feet of Sitka spruce were shipped out of British Columbia, almost seven times recent annual shipments. Despite de Havilland's efforts to use economical laminations of thin pieces of spruce, supplies ran down and Douglas fir had to be enlisted.

Sitka spruce wood is suitable for many uses – interior trim and paneling, house siding and furniture, racing shells, scaffolding and ladders, pulp and paper. For more than six decades, from 1917 until 1980, the vast spruce forests behind Ocean Falls, British Columbia, inundated with an average of 170 inches of rain a year, fed the sawmill, the pulping mill, and the paper-making machines that employed a town full of people.

Sitka spruce reaches its highest pitch in musical instruments, where it is preferred for the tops of violins, bass fiddles, and guitars; the frames of harps; and the sounding boards of pianos. Brian Hoover, an instrument maker on Bowen Island, says Sitka spruce is a unique wood. While light in weight, it won't collapse under the pressure of the strings; the even transition between the darker, harder latewood and the lighter, softer earlywood makes carving easier; it is friendly to the craftsperson because it has no harmful volatile oils; and, most important, it is resonant. Scientists have used laser technology to study the complex vibrational patterns of violin tops but are still mystified that the old craftsmen could predict the tone of a finished instrument. Hoover says he does it just the way Stradivarius did: he taps the wood, listens to the notes it makes, and patiently carves the curves until he gets the right relationship between notes and intervals.

Stradivarius himself used spruce, a cousin of our Sitka spruce but more like Englemann spruce, which also grows in the Pacific Northwest. Reid Hudson, the bowmaker in Duncan, British Columbia, who buys and sells wood for instrument makers, told me of a Montreal violin maker who takes his Sitka spruce-topped instruments to Paris where customers clamor for them. While there he buys European spruce for his Canadian clients who are disdainful of the homegrown wood. Nevertheless, Hudson says, "I don't think any tree sounds better than Sitka spruce." He buys his wood from two salvage loggers

who have been given the right to search in already logged areas on Vancouver Island for windfalls and standing dead trees. They look for a tree that doesn't have branches on the lower reaches of its trunk; one that grows slowly and evenly; and one that doesn't have a corkscrew pattern to its bark, which indicates a slight but undesirable spiral in the fibers of the wood. If it is to produce the top of a double bass, this tree will have to be at least five feet in diameter.

Another craftsman who needs Sitka spruce for a specialized application is Kevin Maher, a Vancouver pilot with a sideline in making wooden canoes and kayaks. But his labor of love is the restoration of a 1936 Boeing Stearman biplane, for which he is constructing a new set of completely wooden wings, using primarily Sitka spruce because it is strong, light, and flexible. For the spars he must have 16-foot lengths of clear wood, six inches wide. He hoards his supply. "It is like gold," he says.

The species is so valuable as an industrial tree that 16 countries are cooperating in what is known as the International Sitka Spruce Provenance Experiment, the results of which will not be known for 30 or 40 years. In countries as widely separated as Australia and Yugoslavia, researchers are taking seed from various places (provenances) and planting them elsewhere to find the genetic material that will produce better trees. In British Columbia researchers have been looking for a faster growing and hardier Sitka spruce. They have found that trees from Oregon and Washington speed upward 40 percent faster when brought to British Columbia and planted in rich soil, but they are, unfortunately, more vulnerable to cold. Quite by chance, the B.C. researchers have grown trees that may help win the ever-continuing battle with *Pissodes strobi*, a weevil that attacks and destroys the vital leading shoot of young Sitka spruce. Seedlings taken from two sites in the province were planted in a high-weevil-hazard area and have proved more resistant to the pest (see "Foes and Friends," page 63).

The British, who have used so much West Coast Sitka spruce, probably know the species as well as North Americans do. Thirty years ago they began an intensive breeding program to improve the vigor, form, and timber quality of the tree, and they once made annual trips to the Pacific Northwest to choose seed that might grow well in locations in Scotland, Wales, and the north of England. Today Sitka spruce is the most important coniferous species in British forestry plantations, and more than a million genetically improved cuttings were planted in Great Britain in 1990.

THE BRITISH MAY PRODUCE their "Super Sitka," but as far as Richard Ring is concerned, nature did that already. In the canopy of the old giant trees, Dr. Ring and his graduate student Neville Winchester are gathering a bounty of insects and have asked world experts to help identify the million specimens of arthropods they have collected. Taxonomists have already named 1,300 species. Sixty-seven have been declared to be definitely new and 300 might be. That is an entomological jackpot. "It's like Christmas Day every day," Ring says.

Despite his excitement, he is trying to steer clear of the insect-of-the-week approach to this research. What he is observing high up in the canopies of the Sitka spruce is an ecosystem where herbivores – tree-munching insects – are kept in control by predators and parasites, such as ladybugs, spiders, and wasps. He sees little in the way of insect damage to the tree and wonders if with greater knowledge we could implement that balance ourselves. The larger lesson is that we have just begun to discover the minute marvels of an ancient forest. "The more information we get," he says, "the better able we will be to avoid the mind-set that we can replant and grow an old-growth forest."

Afterword

SEVERAL YEARS AGO I was sent by a magazine to Holman, a hamlet on Victoria Island in the Canadian Arctic. It was August, a month of blatant floral display in the city, but in Holman all was gray – the ice-filled sea, the foggy sky, and the ubiquitous stones and pebbles on which a few dozen houses sat. When I made this observation to the public health nurse, a woman from the Caribbean, she invited me to walk with her. She took me to a hill of slate and rubble and told me about tiny flowers that grow there early in the summer. She pointed to their remaining leaves, so small I hadn't seen them. Then she handed me stones, drawing my attention to their minute wonders – embedded jewels of a jade color or surface gardens of orange lichen. In a matter of a few minutes this kind woman taught me to see in a new way; it was as though she had reset my eyes so they could focus on the minuscule variations while the larger unvaried landscape blurred into insignificance.

In my time in the forest I have had the same experience. In the beginning I was unable to make distinctions; now I am unable to be among the trees without seeing something entirely new. Today it was what looked like purple, peppercorn-sized berries nestled among the western hemlock needles – a preview of the coming cones. In February, a month before the other conifers were obviously into reproduction, the tips of some western red cedar sprays began to look whiskery while others were topped by tiny black heads – again the first visible manifestations of seed and pollen cones.

Driving is now slightly more risky because I scan tree silhouettes and brake for the unusual. In the process of writing this book, I was often on south Cambie Street in Vancouver where the center boulevard has been planted with a variety of evergreen species. One day, just north of Forty-eighth Avenue, I zipped past a group of conifers, which looked like tall cones of melting wax. Yellow cedars, I thought, as I whipped around the block to check them out. There were three of them – a reminder of the Native legend of the three young women who were tricked by Raven into fleeing from an owl. They ran halfway up a mountain and turned themselves into yellow cedars. I parked and walked over to the trio to get a closer look at the slightly

153

The ever-surprising coastal forest: a red osier dogwood among towering Douglas firs.

flared leaves and the seed cones, about the size of dried currants, but with an unusual pointed protrusion on each scale. I wanted to stop the preoccupied drivers of the rushing cars and tell them about this marvel on Cambie.

A week later, visiting a waterfront property of historical interest here on Bowen Island, I stared in disbelief at a pile of fat green cones about the size of hen's eggs lying on the ground beside a recently felled tree. I picked up sprays of scalelike foliage so prickly it made me wince, and then I counted the 47 annual rings in the red heart-wood and creamy sapwood of what had been a giant sequoia. Astonished at finding a tree of this exotic species on our island, I was saddened to have missed it. But then I noticed three more of them – a grove of giant sequoia on Bowen. Another marvel! The new owners of this property, who believe the previous owner planted those four trees, had removed just one to make room for their house and septic field. I came home with some cones. Within a week the scales had dried and opened, and I was able to tap out the seeds, which I am trying to germinate. Somewhere on our property I shall plant a tree this year – a giant sequoia of this Bowen line perhaps, but a tree of some kind to send into the future for people whose eyes are focused on the marvelous.

ABSCISSION: the separation of flowers, leaves, or fruit from a plant, promoted by a hormone and occurring in a specialized layer of cells.

ANGIOSPERM: a flowering, vascular plant with seeds in a closed ovary (includes broad-leaved trees); an older term for a plant in the botanical division *Magnoliophyta*.

ANNUAL RING: together, the lighter-colored and darker-colored layers of wood laid down by a tree during a year's growth.

ARIL: an exterior covering of some seeds (such as those of the yew) that develops after fertilization.

AXIL: the upper angle between a leaf and the stem from which it arises, or between a branch and trunk.

BOLE: the trunk of a tree.

BOTANICAL ORDER: beginning with the largest and most inclusive, the categories are: division, class, order, family, genus, species, subspecies, and variety. (See *Pinophyta* and *Magnoliophyta*.)

BRACT: a vegetative scale of a cone lying below a seed-bearing scale.

BROAD-LEAVED TREE: a usually deciduous tree (arbutus is one that is evergreen); they are angiosperms, or flowering plants, in the division *Magnoliophyta*.

BRYOPHYTE: nonflowering plants, including mosses, liverworts, and hornworts.

BURL: a hard, woody, roundish growth on the outside of a tree, with irregularly aligned fibers. It may be the result of the growth of buds that appeared where leaves or stems would normally occur.

BUTTRESS: a broadening at the base of a tree or a thickened vertical part of it.

CAMBIUM: a cell layer under the bark; the growing part of a tree that gives rise to new cells.

CANOPY: the combined leaves and branches of the crowns of forest trees.

CATKIN: a hanging spike of petal-less flowers of one sex.

CHLOROPHYLL: green plant pigment important in the production of sugars; a substance that gives green plants their color and allows them to carry on the process of photosynthesis.

CLIMAX FOREST: the last stage in the successional development of a forest in which the composition of the plant community will not change as long as other factors (climate, soil) hold steady.

CLINOMETER: an instrument used to measure angles of elevation or inclination.

CONE: the reproductive organ of conifers, made up of overlapping, spirally arranged scales; male (pollen) cones and female (seed) cones are usually born on the same plant.

CONIFER: a tree or shrub, usually evergreen (but some are deciduous) and usually bearing cones (except yews, which have globular fruit). They may have needlelike or scalelike leaves. Most are in the botanical order *Coniferales*, but yews are in the order *Taxales*. (See *Pinophyta*.)

COTYLEDON: first leaf emerging from a seed.

CROWN: the head of foliage of a tree or shrub.

DECIDUOUS: of a tree, the leaves of which fall off or are shed seasonally or at a certain stage of development in the life cycle.

DENDROCHRONOLOGY: the study of growth rings in trees to determine and date past events, intervals of time, and environmental variations.

DIOCECIOUS: having either staminate (male) or pistillate (female) flowers on different plants. Examples are black cottonwood and Pacific yew.

EARLYWOOD: the softer, more porous portion of an annual ring of wood, produced early in the growing season; also called springwood.

EPICORMIC BRANCH: new shoots that sprout from dormant or sporadically occurring buds on the trunk of a conifer.

EPIPHYTE: a plant that takes its moisture and nutrients from air and rain and usually grows on another plant; includes lichens, liverworts, mosses, and ferns.

FLATSAWN: lumber sawn parallel to a tangent of the growth rings; the face of the board has oval, U- and V-shaped patterns and the annual rings can be seen only on the ends of the boards.

FLUSH: to produce new growth.

GENUS: a category of biological classification, ranking between the family and the species.

GERMINATE: to cause to sprout or develop.

GYMNOSPERM: a plant with naked seeds (for example, most conifers); an older term for seed-bearing plants in the division *Pinophyta*.

HAPLOID: having half the number of chromosomes characteristic of the organism.

HARDWOOD: the wood of a broad-leaved or deciduous tree, or the tree itself.

HEARTWOOD: inner core of a tree trunk, composed primarily of nonliving cells and usually darker in color and denser than the surrounding sapwood.

HYBRID: the offspring of cross-pollinated plants, between two species, varieties, or genera.

LAMMAS GROWTH: a second flushing, which occurs if there is sufficient summer rain and if the tree has been dormant for a relatively short time; Lammas Day is August 1.

LATERAL ROOT: a horizontal root coming from the taproot or the base of the tree.

LATEWOOD: the harder, less porous portion of an annual ring that develops late in the growing season; summerwood.

LAYERING: the formation of roots where a stem touches the ground.

LEADER: the primary or terminal shoot of a tree.

LICHEN: an alga and a fungus growing symbiotically on a surface.

LIGNIN: a polymer in the cell walls of woody tissue that provides rigidity.

MAGNOLIOPHYTA: one of two divisions of seed plants, the members of which bear flowers. An older term, still in use, for these plants is angiosperms. All the broad-leaved trees featured in this book belong to this division. (See *Pinophyta* and botanical order.)

MEGASPORE: a female reproductive cell.

MEIOTIC DIVISION: the cellular process that includes a reduction of chromosomes in cells to the haploid number. It differs from mitotic division in which the two sets of chromosomes are retained.

MICROSPORE: the male spore or pollen grain.

MONOECIOUS: having male and female flowers on the same tree. Most conifers are monoecious.

MYCANGIA: a pouch of the ambrosia beetle that contains fungal spores.

PEDUNCLE: a stalk bearing a flower, flower cluster, fruit, or cone. A leaf stalk is a petiole.

PERFECT: having both stamens and pistils in the same flower; hermaphrodite.

PHLOEM: the inner bark, a pipeline carrying food made in the leaves to the branches, trunk, and roots.

PHOTOSYNTHESIS: a plant process (the reverse of respiration) in which carbohydrate food is synthesized from carbon dioxide and water in chlorophyll-containing tissues exposed to light; oxygen is a by-product of photosynthesis and is released into the atmosphere.

PINOPHYTA: one of the two divisions of seed plants, the members of which are cone-bearing as opposed to flowering. An older term for plants of this type is gymnosperm. All the conifers discussed in this book belong to this division. (See *Magnoliophyta* and botanical classification.)

PITCH: resin from various conifers.

PITH: primary tissue in the central part of a stem, twig, or root; a narrow cylinder of food-storage cells at the center of the heartwood, ascending to the top of the trunk.

POLLINATION: the transfer of pollen from a stamen to a receptive part of the female flower or from the microsporangia in male cones to the ovules in female cones.

POLYGAMOUS: bearing both hermaphrodite (perfect) and unisexual flowers on the same plant.

PROVENANCE: origin, source.

QUARTERSAWN: boards cut from logs that have been sawn into quarters and then cut either in pie-shaped pieces (true quartersawn) or with alternating cuts running parallel to the straight edges of the quarter section (cheated quartersawn). The growth rings can be seen on the ends and running lengthwise on the face of the boards. Also called edgegrain.

RADICLE: root of the seed embryo from which the main root of a tree develops.

RAMICORN BRANCHING: the development, because of a midsummer growth flush, of a second leader, which becomes an upright branch.

RESIN: organic substance bled from trees, usually pines, used in the manufacture of varnish, shellac, and lacquer.

RESPIRATION: the process in plants by which carbohydrates (sugars) and oxygen are combined, releasing carbon dioxide, water, and energy for biochemical cellular processes. The reverse of photosynthesis. It usually occurs when light is not present, but can occur during the day in some plants.

RING SHAKE: a defect in wood caused by shrinkage and separation of the annual rings.

ROOT CROWN: the area where the stem and the root merge.

SAMARA: a key; the dry, closed, usually one-seeded winged fruit of ash, elm, maple.

SAPWOOD: the younger, softer, living or physiologically active outer portion of wood between the cambium and the heartwood; it is more permeable, less durable, and usually lighter in color than the heartwood; it carries water and dissolved minerals from the roots to the leaves.

SCIENTIFIC BINOMIAL: the two Latin terms designating the genus (first) and the specific epithet (second) and together giving the species name.

SELFING: inbreeding, or pollinating of a plant with its own pollen.

SEROTINOUS: cones that stay closed on the tree so that the release of seeds is delayed or occurs gradually.

SHADE TOLERANCE: the ability of a plant to grow in the shade of other plants.

SHOOT: growth sent out by a plant.

SILVICULTURE: a discipline dealing with the establishment, development, reproduction, and care of forest trees.

SOFTWOOD: a conifer or the wood of a conifer, whether it is actually hard or soft.

SPECIES: a logical subclass of a genus, sometimes divided into subspecies.

STOMA (plural, stomata): one of the minute openings in a leaf through which oxygen and carbon dioxide are interchanged with the atmosphere.

STROBILUS: the cone of a gymnosperm. From the Greek *strobilos*, meaning a twisted, whirling object.

SUCCESSION: gradual change in the composition and structure of an ecosystem as organisms (especially the plants) modify their own environment and respond to environmental factors (fire, drought, disease).

TANNIN: a water-soluble compound in certain plants, used in leather tanning and dyeing.

TAPROOT: a large primary root that grows downward, gives off small lateral roots, and provides support.

TAXONOMY: the study of the general principles of scientific classification.

TRANSPIRATION: the passage of watery vapor from a living body through a membrane or pores.

VASCULAR: relating to a tube for conveying fluids in a body. Vascular plants have a specialized conducting system that includes the xylem and phloem.

VEGETATIVE: related to nutritive and growth functions rather than to reproduction.

VERTICAL-CUT: (See quartersawn.)

WHORL: group of more than two leaves, branches, or flowers arranged at the same point on a stem.

WITHE: a tough, slender, flexible branch.

XYLEM: a complex vascular tissue in trees that conducts water and dissolved minerals from the roots to the leaves, stores food, and provides support. It is formed in the growing season by the cambium.

Arno, Stephen F., and Ramona P. Hammerly. *Northwest Trees: Identifying and Understanding the Region's Native Trees*. Seattle: The Mountaineers, 1977.

Carder, Al. *Forest Giants of the World Past and Present*. Markham, ON: Fitzhenry and Whiteside, 1995.

Chaster, G. D., and D. W. Ross and W. H. Warren. *Trees of Greater Victoria: A Heritage*. Victoria: Heritage Tree Book Society, 1988.

Drushka, Ken. *Touch Wood: B.C. Forests at the Crossroads*. Madeira Park, BC: Harbour, 1993.

Farrar, John Laird. *Trees in Canada*. Markham, ON: Fitzhenry and Whiteside and the Canadian Forest Service, 1995.

Hartzell, Hal. *The Yew Tree*. Eugene, OR: Hulogosi, 1991.

Hewes, Jeremy Joan. *Redwoods: The World's Largest Trees*. New York: Gallery, 1984.

Jacobson, Arthur Lee. *Trees of Seattle*. Seattle: Sasquatch, 1989.

Jensen, Edward C., and Charles R. Ross et al. *Trees to Know in Oregon*. Oregon State University Extension Service and Oregon Department of Forestry, 1994.

Kirk, Ruth. *The Olympic Rain Forest: An Ecological Web*. Seattle: U of Washington P, 1992.

Loomis, Ruth, and Merv Wilkinson. *Wildwood: A Forest for the Future*. Gabriola, BC: Reflections, 1990.

Maser, Chris. *Forest Primeval: The Natural History of an Ancient Forest*. Toronto: Stoddart, 1989.

———. *The Redesigned Forest*. Toronto: Stoddart, 1990.

M'Gonigle, Michael, and Ben Parfitt. *Forestopia: A Practical Guide to the New Forest Economy*. Madeira Park, BC: Harbour, 1994.

Moffett, Mark W. *The High Frontier: Exploring the Tropical Rainforest Canopy*. Cambridge, MA: Harvard UP, 1993.

Norse, Elliott A. *Ancient Forests of the Pacific Northwest.*. Washington, DC/Covelo, CA: The Wilderness Society, Island Press, 1990.

Peattie, Donald Culross. *A Natural History of Western Trees*. Boston: Houghton Mifflin, 1953.

Stewart, Hilary. *Cedar: Tree of Life to the Northwest Coast Indians*. Vancouver: Douglas and McIntyre, 1984.

Stoltmann, Randy. *Guide to the Record Trees of British Columbia*. Vancouver: Western Canada Wilderness Committee, 1993.

Straley, Gerald B. *Trees of Vancouver: A Guide to the Common and Unusual Trees of the City*. Vancouver: U of British Columbia P, 1992.

Van Pelt, Robert. *Washington Big Tree Program 1994*. Seattle: U of Washington P, 1994.

159

Page numbers referring to photographs and captions are in italics.

and decomposition, 144; density of forest of, 134; as fiber source in manufacturing, 128; and forest succession, 132, 134; habitat of, 132; Native uses of, 134; needles of, 2; and nurse logs, 135-36; seed cones of, *111*; seedling of, *133*; and windthrow, 135

western red cedar (*Thuja plicata*), *66*, *67*, *71*; and aging, 67, 77-78; bark of, 75; classification of, 77; and climate, 78; compared with yellow cedar, 82; distribution of, 77; foliage of, 2, *76*, 77, *80*; future of, 79-80; and genetic variation, 78; and grizzly bear, *72-73*; habitat of, 77-78; Native epithets for, 77; Native uses of, 70, 74; seed cones of, 77; seed production of, 111;

and self-pollination, 78-79; totem poles made from, *68-69*; uses for wood of, 79-80

white redwood, 18

Wildwood Tree Farm, 6

Wilkinson, Merv, 6

Willamette Mission State Park (Oregon), 90

Wind River Experimental Forest, 124

Woods, Jack, 38, 41, 42, 110

yellow cedar (*Chamaecyparis nootkatensis*), *83*; age of, 82; compared with western red cedar, 82; foliage of, 82; habitat of, 81; range of, 81-82; reproduction of, 82; and true cedars, 81; uses for wood of, 82